"If you feel like you are stuck in a rut, John Siebeling's book *Momentum* will give you the spiritual traction to move forward with the life that God has for you to live."

> Craig Groeschel
> senior pastor, LifeChurch.tv
> author of *Soul Detox: Clean Living in a Contaminated World*

"When you feel stuck, everything in your life seems like a dead end. You start to wonder: will I be in this job forever? Will my marriage ever get better? Will this debt ever be paid? We've all felt stuck at some point in our lives, but it doesn't have to be that way! By living life God's way, we can move forward. Read *Momentum* and get unstuck!"

> Greg Surratt
> lead pastor, Seacoast Church; author of *Ir-rev-rend*

"Simply put, *Momentum* is a powerful, profound, and truly inspiring work by one of my very favorite pastors. I know Pastor John personally, and I'm telling you, no one has a bigger heart for helping people find freedom and purpose. He's the "real deal"! If you feel stuck in a rut, battling the same issues year after year, or simply at odds with God's will for your life, you need this book. It will change your life forever!"

> Nancy Alcorn
> founder and president, Mercy Ministries

"Pastor John Siebeling brilliantly highlights the five dynamics of divine momentum. On these pages you'll discover that everything you need to move forward has been woven into the Lord's Prayer. Read it and move forward!"

> John and Lisa Bevere
> authors/speakers
> Messenger International, Colorado/Australia/United Kingdom

"I think *Momentum* has the potential to help a great number of people overcome the obstacles that are slowing them down in life. This book takes a practical look at the Lord's Prayer and the change that's possible when we make it more than just words we say and let it be a way of life. John guides the reader through the Lord's Prayer, identifying the biblical principles found in it and explaining them in a way that is easy to understand. I believe that as these principles are put into action, your life can't help but move forward!"

> Tommy Barnett
> senior pastor, Phoenix First founder, Los Angeles Dream Center

"This book from John is long overdue. Momentum is an elusive thing. When you are in it, everything is so easy. When you are not, everything can feel very hard. John has a real revelation on how to do what is needed to get in the flow."

> David Meyer
> CEO, Hand of Hope; co-overseer, Joyce Meyer Ministries

"We all desperately need momentum to get past our past and to experience God's preferred future for our lives. Pastor John gives five powerful, life-changing principles that will be a catalyst to you experiencing momentum in your life!"

Herbert Cooper, lead pastor, People's Church

"If you are looking for momentum in your life, this book is a must-read. Pastor Siebeling will give you the inspiration and information you need to move forward in your life. Both practical truths and spiritual power are communicated through the pages of *Momentum*. The well-known Lord's Prayer will take on brand-new meaning for you and you'll be lifted, encouraged, and empowered to move forward in the life that God has for you."

Dr. Casey Treat
senior pastor, Christian Faith Center

"Momentum can be our best friend and greatest ally. The absence of positive momentum can make the challenges we face in life even more daunting. John Siebeling's *Momentum* is an inspiring book full of great stories, powerful insights, and relatable truths. I highly recommend the man and the message. You'll want to buy this book and get one for a friend—it will get your life moving in the right direction."

Philip Wagner
lead pastor, Oasis Church in Los Angeles;
author of *How to Turn Your Marriage Around in 10 Days*

"Every time I am with John Siebeling, I walk away encouraged and challenged. The five key principles in this book are not pie-in-the-sky theories, but biblical fact that has been walked out in shoe leather by John Siebeling himself. Are you ready for a life change? Is it time to gain some momentum and break out of that rut? Then dive in to my friend's book."

Scott R. Jones
senior pastor, Grace Church, Houston, Texas
chairman, Global Network of Christian Ministries

"*Momentum* is a book that will encourage the reader to not only walk in God's favor but also to thrive in the amazing future that he has planned for them. I truly believe that the principles covered here are the core values of what keeps a Christian growing in their walk with God. John Siebeling has such a relatable and inspiring writing style that will connect with believers new and old alike. I would highly recommend this book to anybody who would like to restore their focus on God from the inside out, and to surge forward into a future of unimaginable blessings."

Pastor Matthew Barnett, cofounder of the Dream Center

MOMENTUM

FIVE KEYS FROM THE LORD'S PRAYER
TO GETTING UNSTUCK
AND *MOVING FORWARD*

JOHN SIEBELING

BakerBooks
a division of Baker Publishing Group
Grand Rapids, Michigan

© 2013 by John Siebeling

Published by Baker Books
a division of Baker Publishing Group
P.O. Box 6287, Grand Rapids, MI 49516-6287
www.bakerbooks.com

Printed in the United States of America

Library of Congress Cataloging-in-Publication Data is on file at the Library of Congress, Washington, DC.

ISBN 978-0-8010-1504-5 (pbk.)

13 14 15 16 17 18 19   7 6 5 4 3 2 1

I dedicate this book to family . . .

First, the amazing family God started in my life when he gave me Leslie. I would not be who I am today if it weren't for her and her love and commitment to me throughout the years. And to Anna and Mark, our two incredible children, who have taught me a lot about life and have given me joy beyond measure.

Second, my incredible church family, The Life Church. You have loved me, followed me, believed in me, listened to me, and lived out the keys of momentum described here.

Contents

Foreword

The Lord's Prayer might be one of the most venerated passages in all of Scripture. Yet, it is possible that these recognizable words have lost their potency in our hearts. We quote it over meals and during church services, before bed and first thing in the morning, but somehow the power behind the passage has gotten swept underneath the rug of familiarity.

Pastor John has lifted up the carpet and reintroduced this gem of Scripture in a relevant way that is sure to reignite your desire for abundant living. He writes the same way he lives—openly, authentically, practically, and powerfully.

Years before he crafted this book, he prayerfully shaped a thriving and vibrant church in what has historically been known as one of the most racially torn cities in America. Together with his wife Leslie, he has championed the causes of Christ and has called his neighbors to do the same. The Life Church sits as a poignant beacon of light, piercing the surrounding darkness of poverty and crime with a clarion call to victorious living . . . and action.

It only takes a few seconds to see the obvious effects of this church's mission. As soon as you walk through the front door, you are greeted by a multiethnic, multigenerational, multidimensional church that doesn't sit on its haunches listening to God's Word, singing a few songs, and then heading off mindlessly to Sunday brunch. This congregation serves. They exchange their suits and ties, dresses and high heels for T-shirts, tennis shoes, and backpacks full of love that they can dispense in practical ways to the homeless and hungry, marginalized and lonely. Christ's message is not just *heard* here, it is *seen*.

That's why this book is so valuable. Every word and every chapter is steeped in a level of insight that can't be learned on even the most astute university campus. This kind of revelation can only come from an individual who is a mission-hearted, family-oriented, church-erecting, passionate Jesus follower who has traded in the well-trodden road of half-heartedness for the narrow pathway of abundant life. And this book is our invitation to come along for the ride.

John's not just going to tell us what we should do, he's going to show us *how* to do it. Every section will masterfully capture your attention through personal stories that will pique your interest and intelligence and then, like a drill mining for the finest of jewels, it will dive into the depths of your soul with a life-altering principle that will reshape your thinking and then your life. Having a life fueled by divine momentum is not a mission impossible after all. Not if Pastor John Siebeling has anything to do with it.

Let's be honest, there aren't enough Christians experiencing the victorious life of Christ, and there are too few churches serving the purposes outlined by Christ. If the enemy has his way, God's people would slip down a strategically designed slope of spiritual decay until we are powerless and ineffective. But the inspired writings in this book will put an end to that scheme . . . if the church takes hold of it. I believe she will. I believe *we will*.

So, turn the page, my friend, and get ready for a reacquaintance with the Lord's Prayer that will change your life forever.

Priscilla Shirer

Acknowledgments

A huge thank you to . . .

Aimee and Katie—for countless hours planning, writing, editing, thinking, etc. No way this book would have been done without you!

Tom—for your insight and helping me to get a book published.

Dudley—for all you contributed as this book took shape and for your perspective along the way.

Jon and the Baker team—for your feedback and for your guidance through this process.

Pastors Don and Amy—for pouring into Leslie and me over the years and for teaching and living out so many of the principles found in this book. Leslie and I love you.

The Life Church staff and team—for your relentless passion and hard work to help people meet Jesus and move forward into all he has for their lives. Thanks for supporting the vision and for building a world-class church.

Introduction

Getting Unstuck

I seldom end up where I wanted to go, but almost always end up where I need to be.

Douglas Adams

Sweat trickled down my back as I steered the van along a dusty African road. Around us, the Serengeti spread in every direction like an emerald sea, dotted here and there by an acacia tree or a grazing herd of elephants. We had been to the Maasai Mara Game Reserve, one of the world's most amazing ecosystems, and were on our way back to Nairobi.

At the time, my wife, Leslie, and I were serving on the staff of a church there. My sister had come from the States for a visit and wanted to see the sights. We were eager to show off our newfound familiarity with all things African, and a tour of the game reserve seemed like just the thing. We came away in awe of the exotic animals we saw roaming in their natural habitat.

While Kenya has modern cities with paved streets, electricity, and all the comfort Westerners expect, outside those urban areas lie some of the most remote regions in the world. The road we were on that day snaked a treacherous trail through the grassy plains. With potholes that seemed as big as our van and rocks that could shred a tire or puncture a radiator, the route required my best concentration. As the sun beat down on us, I kept my eyes focused intently on the road ahead.

About an hour out of Narok, the largest town nearby, we came upon a young Maasai boy just a few yards from the road. He wore nothing but a loincloth and carried a walking stick that he used to tend a herd of cows as they grazed near the road. The scene was like a picture from *National Geographic*, and I watched him as we rode past. Huge mistake! Just as I returned my attention to the dirt road, we ran straight into a jagged rock.

I hit the brakes, and the thump beneath my feet told me we had almost cleared the rock. *Almost.* The rising temperature gauge on the dash displayed that almost wasn't good enough. Coasting to the narrow shoulder, I brought the van to a stop and got out to survey the damage. As I raised the hood, steam rose in the air and I saw green iridescent liquid dripping from the bottom of the radiator. All the coolant pooled beneath the van on the hot, dirt road. We wouldn't be going anywhere soon.

We were stuck.

Sooner or Later

The Serengeti offers unbelievable beauty—it's the kind of place where you can sit for hours watching the grass sway in the breeze, ebbing and flowing like ocean waves. At night, with no urban glare to hide them, the stars cover the sky and seem to glow like a cosmic lamppost. But right then, on the side of that road, with the coolant from the van seeping into the soft soil of the African savanna, that landscape looked ominous and imposing. We were stuck, and I couldn't see how we were going to get moving again.

Walking really wasn't an option. As much as we had tried to learn the culture and blend in, we were still white in a land populated by dark-skinned people. A white man with two white women, on a lonely stretch of backcountry road in southwestern Kenya, provided a target too tempting for bandits. And how long would we have to walk in the stifling heat before we reached Narok? At least by staying with the van we would have some protection from the sun. So we decided to wait, trusting that sooner or later someone would come along.

After almost an hour of making nervous small talk, Leslie noticed a cloud of dust to the south of us. "Someone's coming," she said. The tone of her voice alerted me to the tension we all were feeling. An approaching vehicle could be good news, someone to help. Or it could be a truckload of thieves on their way to rob us.

"Please, Lord," I prayed, "let it be help." I stepped out of the van as a safari vehicle pulled to a stop beside us. The driver was Kenyan. Rolling the window down, he didn't say a word. My gut tightened, and I shaded my eyes with my hand.

"Can you help us?" I asked.

He was driving a group of Australian tourists back to Nairobi, and they cheerfully agreed to let us hitch a ride. Relieved beyond measure, we locked our van and jumped aboard. Thank God for the Aussies!

Cooking Lessons

An hour later, we arrived in Narok hot and sweaty but glad to be back in civilization. After a snack and a Diet Coke, I set out in search of a mechanic to repair the van. Leslie and my sister Kathy stayed back at the café inside the Spear Hotel. It wasn't much by American standards, but it was much more pleasant than returning to the van and quite a bit safer.

Thanks to the hotel staff, I located someone who said he could repair the radiator and a driver with a car to get us back to where we'd left our van. Momentarily excited, my confidence wilted when I saw what the mechanic brought with him in the way of tools: a jug of water to refill the radiator and a box of something he said would fix the leak. The three of us set out to find the van, and I started praying again.

As we left town, the driver confirmed what I'd already heard. Earlier that week bandits had found a carload of tourists stranded on the side of the road. They had robbed the visitors and then stripped them of their clothes. Kenya, for all its advances, could be a dangerous place.

After what seemed like forever, we rounded a bend in the road, and, much to my relief, I saw the van still parked where I had left it and with all four tires still in place. The mechanic raised the hood, checked the hoses, and pointed to the bottom of the radiator. "That is your problem," he said, stating the obvious. "There's a hole in it. All the fluid leaked out."

"Can you fix it?"

"Oh yes." He nodded. He set the jug of water on the ground and took the container of repair material from the box.

My heart sank when I saw it was a box of Royco—a waxy cornstarch used for cooking. "*That*'s what you brought? Cooking powder?"

"Oh yes," he said. "It works for many things." He added water and mixed it into a thick paste, then dumped it into the radiator.

There goes that, I thought to myself. We would have to buy a new radiator. And who knows how long that would take.

The mechanic gave me a triumphant smile. "Now we wait."

While the waxy paste settled into the radiator, all I could do was sit and worry. The mechanic and our driver sprawled across their seats like they didn't have a care in the world and dozed in the afternoon heat. Finally, the mechanic, refreshed from his nap, climbed out and emptied his water jug into the radiator. Seeing him motion for me to crank the engine, I turned the key and held my breath. The engine sprang to life!

While it was a relief to hear it running, I knew the real test was whether the "patch" would hold when the water got hot. The needle on the temperature gauge steadily rose before hovering in the mid-range operating level. So far, so good—but would it get us back to Nairobi?

Thankfully, we made it out of the Serengeti on that trip to the game reserve. Not only did the cornstarch patch for the radiator get us back to the city, but it also held long enough for me to find a garage and have the radiator permanently repaired. Who knew?

Fantastic Five

Maybe you're facing situations right now that have you wondering if you'll ever get past them. Thankfully, God hasn't left us on our own to figure them out. He has given us a step-by-step guide for living a life that's successful, as he defines success (which is far greater than how we tend to define it), and full of significance. We find this guide in the prayer Jesus taught his disciples, the Lord's Prayer, one of the most familiar passages in Scripture. Many of us know it by heart.

Jesus offered this prayer as a pattern to help us pray effectively and align ourselves with the heart of our Father. This prayer also contains keys for daily living. When we put them into action, they can impact the practical aspects of our lives, as well as our relationship with God, and create forward momentum.

Here's a quick look at the five keys that can help us get unstuck and move our lives forward.

Honor: living a standout life
Renewal: allowing God to change you from the inside out

16

Release: breaking barriers to receive God's blessings

Forgiveness: living by God's grace and extending it to others

Pursuit: aligning yourself with God's plan for your life

These five principles are God's prescription for living life to the fullest. When applied to our everyday lives, they serve as catalysts of change that will move us toward a life lived to the fullest—an abundant life fueled by purpose and significance and brimming with joy and peace.

A Way Forward

Maybe you haven't been stuck on the side of the road in Africa, but I'll bet you can relate. On any given day, many of us wrestle with feeling overwhelmed and under-resourced for the problems we face. Some of these problems linger and over time begin to weigh on us. Maybe it's a sense of helpless frustration in a job you don't enjoy, a lifelong dream that always remains out of reach, or a mountain of debt weighing you down. Perhaps it's a relationship that isn't going how you thought it would or a bad habit you just can't seem to kick. Maybe you simply find yourself wondering if there's more to life than what you're experiencing now.

For every step forward, it seems there are two steps back. The past can't be undone, and yet you can't envision how the future will be any different. You feel stuck in the middle of your own life. You want to change, you long to grow, you sense there's more to life than what you've settled for. But like someone lost in the woods without a compass, you're just not sure which direction leads you home.

You may feel frustrated and immobilized, even paralyzed. You may be dealing with anger and hurt from the past. Or you may be fairly content with your life but still have a lingering goal or dream that you have yet to see fulfilled. Or perhaps you feel tired and discouraged. You've tried everything you know to do but with no results. No matter where you find yourself, there's a way to regain your momentum and get your life moving again in a positive direction.

Even though you've probably prayed it before, I encourage you to pray the Lord's Prayer right now, asking God to give you fresh eyes to see his truth in a new way. Consider what you're really praying, what you're asking God to do in your life, and allow the words to come from your heart. Think about how you want to change. And get ready to see momentum come into your life!

"Our Father in heaven, hallowed be your name, your kingdom come, your will be done on earth as it is in heaven. Give us today our daily bread. Forgive us our debts, as we also have forgiven our debtors. And lead us not into temptation, but deliver us from the evil one" (Matt. 6:9–13).

KEY 1

HONOR

LIVING A STANDOUT LIFE

1

Made of Honor

Our Father in heaven, hallowed be your name.

Matthew 6:9

One Sunday after church, when I was about ten years old, my father took me to pick up some fried chicken for lunch. We went to a hole-in-the-wall café called Bonaparte's near our house. It was a greasy spoon, but they had the best fried chicken in town.

When we arrived, there was a line of customers out the door. The summer air was hot, the air conditioner in the restaurant was obviously broken, and only one person, an older African American woman, was working the counter. We took our place in line, and the smell of chicken frying made my mouth water. I only wished we'd come earlier to beat the crowd.

Ladies in line fanned themselves, many still dressed up from church. A couple of men talked baseball, while a young family waited to be seated. As the wait continued and the heat became unbearable, people began to complain. It started with typical comments like, "Didn't they know we'd be here?" and "Can't they remember lunch comes at the same time every day?"

I heard what they said but didn't pay much attention. My dad was not a patient person by nature, and I could tell he wasn't happy about having to wait either, but he bit his tongue. Then the guy behind us, who'd been grumbling for some time already, called out to the woman at the counter, "Hey, *girl*! Think you could move a little faster?"

My father's demeanor changed in an instant.

My dad was a professor of immunology at Louisiana State University, teaching and conducting research at the lab. And he pretty much looked the part. He was exactly what you think of when you picture a scientist who spends most of his time in a laboratory.

In that moment, when the customer behind us became disrespectful, my dad rose up in the most powerful way I'd ever witnessed. In my eyes as a ten-year-old, he instantly became the strongest, most heroic man I'd ever known.

"Now that's *enough*," he said firmly, turning to face the guy. "We're all hot. The line is long. The wait is aggravating, but there's no reason for you to talk to her like that."

My father's jaw was tense, his eyes focused, and I had never seen him look so intense. The other guy was solidly built and looked like he'd already gone a few rounds with the last person who'd gotten in his way. I remember standing in that line, being sure there was going to be a fight. From the way the crowd reacted—with lots of murmurs and steps back—I think everyone else thought the same thing.

The two men stared at each other for what seemed like hours until finally the other guy snarled and looked away. We all breathed a sigh of relief, but everyone in the room, including me, understood that there had been a silent battle of sorts that took place in that moment between my dad and that man. I didn't fully understand why, but I could tell that it had been a pretty big deal. When we got up to the counter to order, the lady silently mouthed "Thank you" to my dad.

On the ride home, my father explained to me what had really happened back at the restaurant. It was the late 1970s, and while the South was changing, terms such as *boy* and *girl* were still used by some white people as put-downs of African Americans.

That's what the customer at Bonaparte's had meant, and all the other adults there knew it. When my dad stood up to the guy in line, he wasn't just standing up to a bully or taking up for the woman behind the counter. He was standing up for the value God has instilled in each and every person he created. It wasn't easy, it may not have been popular, and it made both of us (and a lot of other people) uncomfortable. But my dad knew what was right, and he stood up for it. To him, it was a matter of honor.

We are to be people of honor. This is sometimes a foreign concept in our society, but honor is the foundation of the plan that God gives us for connecting to God in prayer, and an important part of moving our lives forward.

Honor for God should always translate into being a person of honor and showing honor to others. We'll talk more about that specifically later, but the point that's illustrated in this story is that honor is something that you will eventually have to take a stand for. It is a character trait or a value that requires action. It can't be passive. My father could have said that he honored and valued people of different races, but if he had failed to stand up for her, there wouldn't have been much credibility to his words. The same is true when it comes to honoring God. Honoring God is going to require that we stand out in the world around us sometimes because of what we believe and how we choose to act as a result.

Honorable Mention

The concept that we should treat God with reverence, honor, and respect is clearly prevalent throughout the Bible. The Lord's

Prayer is no exception and, in fact, begins with, "Our Father in heaven, *hallowed* be your name." Now, if you're like me, you've prayed that prayer many times without really thinking about what the word *hallowed* actually means. I had to look it up.

The word *hallowed* means to set apart as holy, to respect something and honor it greatly. *Webster's Dictionary*, circa 1913, defines honor as a "manifestation of respect or reverence . . . excellence of character; high moral worth; virtue; nobleness."

Now, I know those aren't words we use much today, but I like going back to a definition from a book that was written a hundred years ago. There are a lot of different aspects and nuances to the word *honor*, but perhaps my favorite definition of honor as it relates to honoring God is this: esteem paid to the worth of something. In this context, to honor something means to regard it with the level of value and respect that it deserves or requires because of its inherent worth. This is the kind of honor that the Lord's Prayer is talking about when it says "hallowed be your name." Jesus understood how incredible, majestic, and powerful his Father God was, and the exceptional honor indicated by the word *hallowed* was a response to that greatness and worth.

Fighting for Freedom

Of the five keys we find in the Lord's Prayer, honor stands alone in that it's the one principle that is completely up to us. Most of the prayer involves us requesting something from God—for his kingdom to come, for forgiveness of our sins, for provision of our daily bread, and for his leading and deliverance in our lives. And though we do have a responsibility and a part to play in those things, honor is something that *we* bring God when we go to him in prayer. As Jesus approaches God in this model prayer, before he asks for anything, he brings honor to his Father.

Part of honor is surrendering our will and pledging our devotion and loyalty to something we regard as greater than ourselves. Even if it comes at the price of personal sacrifice.

Honor is something that causes our lives to stand out from the crowd—it moves us to step up and take action because we value something so strongly and so highly. This always makes me think of one of my favorite movies, *Braveheart*, an epic tale about William Wallace. His life was devoted to the cause of freedom for his people. It's gut-wrenching, inspiring, and stirs up something inside me each time I watch it.

I love the part of the movie when Wallace is addressing his men and asking them to choose whether or not they will join him in his cause to fight for freedom. He challenges them with this powerful statement: "They may take our lives, but they'll never take our freedom!" He had a conviction so strong inside him that it held him to a course of action—one that ultimately required his life. But it was a price he was willing to pay for the cause he believed in. It all came down to honor.

We should have some convictions that we are so committed to that we're willing to pay a great price to uphold them. William Wallace was willing to stand up for justice and give his life for the freedom of his country; how much more should we be willing to take a stand for God and honor him with our lives? Wallace's cause had earthly value, but if we serve God, we are part of a cause that has eternal value as well as earthly value. We have something far greater to live our lives for and take a stand for. Honor for God is the greatest conviction we can possess, and it's the starting point for a life that's moving forward in the right direction.

Fighting for Honor

"Hallowed be your name" is more than just a phrase we pray; it has to be the way we *live*. David is a great example of this. As a young boy, he was given the task of caring for his father's flocks of sheep. He was the youngest of eight brothers and probably fell lowest in the ranks of importance in the family. He was stuck out in the pastures with the sheep while his three oldest brothers went off to war.

One day his father tells him to take supplies to the battlefield and find out how his brothers are doing. When David arrives, he immediately sets out to find them. The Bible says that as David and his brothers are talking, the Philistine champion Goliath shows up, saying what he'd been saying twice a day for forty days: "I defy the armies of Israel this day; give me a man, that we may fight together" (1 Sam. 17:10 NKJV). Goliath was the most honored of the Philistines, and he struck fear in the hearts of the Israelite warriors. "When they saw the man, [they] fled from him and were dreadfully afraid" (1 Sam. 17:24 NKJV).

In that moment, David sees everyone he respects retreating. He sees seasoned warriors, the king's forces, turning their backs and running for their lives. David is outraged! He asks, "What shall be done for the man who kills this Philistine and takes away the reproach from Israel? For who is this uncircumcised Philistine, that he should defy the armies of the living God?" (1 Sam. 17:26 NKJV).

David has a sense of honor for God that the others lack. When everyone else turns and runs, honor causes David to stand his ground and step up for what he believes. He goes to Saul and tells him not to worry—that he is going to fight Goliath. Can you imagine how bold and gutsy it was for a young shepherd boy to go to the king and tell him this when all the trained warriors had fled? David's oldest brother had already told him that he had no business being there (1 Sam. 17:28). And when David approaches Saul again, a second time, David's bold statement is met with a negative response. Saul tells him, "You are not able to go against this Philistine to fight with him; for you are a youth, and he a man of war from his youth" (1 Sam. 17:33 NKJV).

David is undeterred. He responds, "Your servant has killed both lion and bear; and this uncircumcised Philistine will be like one of them, seeing he has defied the armies of the living God." David goes on to say, "The LORD, who delivered me from the paw of the lion and from the paw of the bear, He will deliver me from the hand of this Philistine" (1 Sam. 17:36–37 NKJV).

So Saul sends him out. David prepares his sling and his stones and goes out to meet the mighty giant.

What happens next is truly amazing. While everyone else has cowered and retreated, David rushes *toward* Goliath. While others have moved *backward*, David moves *forward*. His courage and fearlessness were rooted in his high view of God and the uncompromising trust it produced in his heart. In the moment of decision, David had the strength and boldness to *run forward* when everyone else was retreating.

From the moment he heard Goliath's defiant words, something rose up within David. He was moved to stand up for the honor of the God he served. In the face of what others considered impossible odds and certain failure, David's honor for God was louder than any other voice in his life. Honor for God overwhelmed emotions of fear, thoughts of failure, his brother's disdain, and the king's doubt. When David heard Goliath dishonor God, it incited a holy passion and conviction within him that compelled him to take action.

Honor has the power to ignite something significant inside us when it's attached to a worthy cause. When his brother tried to hold him back, telling him he belonged with the sheep and asking him why he had even bothered to come, David gave a powerful reply: "Is there not a cause?" He knew he was fighting for more than just the fame associated with defeating an enemy no one else dared to fight. David attached his life to the greatest cause there is: living for the honor of the one true God. His life was devoted to loving, serving, and honoring God for one reason: "that all the earth may know that there is a God in Israel" (1 Sam. 17:46). A life of honor attracts the favor of God and brings momentum into our lives.

Clothed with Honor

In Psalm 104, we see that honor for God was a hallmark of David's life and the foundation for his praise:

> Bless the LORD, O my soul!
>
> O LORD my God, You are very great:
> You are clothed with honor and majesty,
> Who cover Yourself with light as with a garment,
> Who stretch out the heavens like a curtain.
>
> He lays the beams of His upper chambers in the waters,
> Who makes the clouds His chariot,
> Who walks on the wings of the wind,
> Who makes His angels spirits,
> His ministers a flame of fire.
>
> You who laid the foundations of the earth,
> So that it should not be moved forever,
> You covered it with the deep as with a garment;
> The waters stood above the mountains.
> At Your rebuke they fled;
> At the voice of Your thunder they hastened away.
> (Ps. 104:1–7 NKJV)

What an awesome picture of God—full of power and authority and majesty! He laid the very foundations of the earth. Stop and think about that! How tall are the mountains and how deep are the oceans? Consider how deep the Grand Canyon is. You may think the bottom is close to the foundations of the earth, but even in its extreme depths the Grand Canyon is really just a little crack on the earth's surface. God is a God who is amazing beyond what our finite minds can even begin to understand.

Forward Favor

When we see God for who he is, we can't help but be filled with awe and wonder and moved to honor. David wasn't perfect, but clearly he had a revelation of God's magnificence. He chose to honor God *above all else*. Honor for God was the primary and defining force at work in his life.

Honor moved David to action—bold, courageous action birthed out of conviction. The all-consuming honor and respect he had for God gave him the strength and audacity to stand up for what he valued. He fought Goliath so "that all the earth may know that there is a God in Israel." Honor for his God moved him to take on the impossible—and he prevailed!

Honor catapulted David into a whole new life as well. As a result of his triumph over the giant, he was launched into a new sphere of influence. He went from being the annoying little brother who was stuck in the fields with the sheep to being the nation's hero. David eventually became the greatest king his people ever had and was listed in the genealogy of Jesus.

Honoring God may not instantly propel us to a place of fame and prominence, but I do know this: A person who is committed to the honor of God will move forward in life. While we may not move forward on the world's terms, we can be confident that God looks favorably on those who honor him. The rewards of a God-honoring life are far greater than anything this world can offer.

Just like David we will likely face some opposition and resistance when we choose to honor God, but honor for the greatest of causes will keep us pressing forward in the face of difficulty. It will take us beyond a going-through-the-motions type of life and position us for a life of significance. Honor was the difference between David and Israel's warriors. God is looking for people whose lives have an extraordinary level of honor for him. And what I've found is that opportunities for extraordinary honor aren't limited to life's battlefields. If we'll open our eyes, we'll find opportunities for extraordinary honor in the ordinary moments of our everyday lives.

2

Honor Code

> No person was ever honored for what he
> received. Honor has been the reward for
> what he gave.
>
> Calvin Coolidge

A few years ago, I was reading some stats about Memphis, the city where I live and the city that I love. It's the birthplace of rock 'n' roll, the home of Elvis and his beloved Graceland, and a significant location in the Civil Rights movement, not to mention that it has incredible barbeque and blues music.

Unfortunately, though, Memphis ranks at the top of lists you don't want to be on—poverty, crime, bankruptcy—and is sadly the infant mortality capital of the United States. Then I read another stat that stopped me in my tracks: In some Memphis zip codes, as many as 74 percent of children go to bed hungry each night. I couldn't believe that twenty minutes from my house many kids were not eating at night and were lying in bed with rumbling stomachs.

I found out from teachers that many kids go to school hungry, devour the breakfast and lunch provided by the school, and then don't eat again until they go back the next morning. That disturbed me.

A week or so after reading those stats, I heard Pastor Tommy Barnett from Phoenix speak. I've always admired the phenomenal ministry that he and his son started with the Dream Center in Los Angeles. It's an innovative place that feeds the hungry, provides recovery programs, and helps restore broken people. After hearing Pastor Tommy's message I left inspired and made a commitment in my heart that our church wouldn't let any child go to bed hungry in Memphis.

Some of our church staff and key volunteers researched options for quite awhile, but we struggled to know how to tackle such a massive need. Before we knew it, a year had passed and we still didn't have a plan of action.

About a year later, I heard Pastor Tommy's son Matthew preach at a conference. He's become a good friend of ours over the years, and as I sat and listened to him share so passionately that night about reaching people, I knew we couldn't wait any longer.

Keep On Truckin'

Shortly after the conference, Matthew Barnett came to speak at our church. He shared some of the most incredible stories of life transformation as he talked about what was taking place through the Dream Center. At the end of the night, I talked with him about our dilemma and how to start feeding needy kids in our community. Immediately, he smiled at me and said enthusiastically, "This is what you do. Buy some delivery trucks and refurbish them. Try to get some food donated and then partner with the schools in the area with the greatest need. Make up bags for each child, drive the trucks to the schools, and when the kids are leaving school, give them food." That sounded like something we could do. I went home that night knowing we had found our plan of action.

A few weeks later I told the church our plan. People were so moved by the plight of hungry kids in Memphis that a wave of spontaneous generosity broke out. People came up to me after services with checks in hand, some even for the full amount needed to purchase a truck. Within a few months, we had distributed over forty-eight thousand meals, and in less than a year, we were feeding over seventeen hundred hungry kids! Every Friday, teams go out with our trucks to distribute bags of food in the areas of greatest need. There are many more hungry mouths to feed, but it's an awesome start to helping our city.

As a result, our church has gained respect and influence in Memphis. The impact is so far beyond what we could have done on our own that it can only be attributed to God moving on our behalf. Here's the key: We made a commitment to honor God by taking care of people in our city who are in need, and as a result, respect and momentum have flowed back to us. This isn't a coincidence. In the Bible, we discover an amazing result of honoring God—one so bold you may have a hard time believing it. *When you honor God, he honors you.*

Honor in Action

I know it may sound a little audacious to think that God honors us. It may sound presumptuous or even prideful. Could it really be possible that the God of the universe would honor us human beings? Based on what God says in his Word, the answer is clearly yes! "I will honor those who honor me" (1 Sam. 2:30 NLT).

If you want to receive honor from God, then you must show him honor. As I have studied the Bible, I have found that there are three significant ways we should honor God:

1. We should honor God with our finances.
2. We should honor God by honoring his house (the local church).
3. We should honor God by honoring people.

Money Matters

"Honor the LORD with your wealth and with the best part of everything you produce" (Prov. 8:9 NLT).

Clearly, if we're going to honor God, we have to honor him with our money. The Bible tells us that where a man's treasure is, there his heart will be also (Matt. 6:21). God doesn't need our money, but he does want our hearts. He wants to be first place in our hearts and in our lives. If God is first in our lives, it will translate into how we handle our money.

I think for many people, generosity is a missing link to momentum. When we're generous, it makes a difference in the lives of others but also in our own lives. Proverbs 11:24–25 tells us, "The world of the generous gets larger and larger; the world of the stingy gets smaller and smaller. The one who blesses others is abundantly blessed; those who help others are helped" (Message).

To me, generosity has a face. I see my good friends Pete and Kristi, who decided to drive an older car for another year so they could give more to our church's expansion initiatives. I picture Denzel, a teenager who sold cinnamon rolls and cookies every Wednesday to raise money for his friend Tim to go to Joplin, Missouri, to help rebuild the city after a devastating tornado. I remember Lydia, who at sixteen didn't buy a car with her savings so she could go to Africa and serve. I think of Kyle, who didn't take a promotion at work in order to keep serving a significant number of hours each week on the worship team at church.

These are everyday people who are finding ways to value God and his work above all else. We don't have to have a lot of money to honor God with it—it's our attitude and what we do with our money that matter to God.

What keeps you from giving as generously as possible from your financial resources? Are you afraid you won't have enough? I encourage you to make a shift in your thinking and in your perspective. Take a step of faith and choose to honor God by being generous with your finances. It's really an attitude that spans the breadth of our lives—from our perspective on money, to giving to the needy, to how we tip servers.

An openhanded mind-set will build much more momentum in our lives than a stingy spirit will. However God chooses to honor us, what flows back into our lives, whether tangible or intangible, will always outweigh the sacrifice we made. Sometimes honoring him is costly, but the respect and honor we release to God never go unnoticed or unreturned by our Father.

House Party

"Lord, I love the house where you live, the place where your glory dwells" (Ps. 26:8).

Second, the Bible is very clear that we honor God by honoring his house. "God's house" is another term for the local church (1 Tim. 3:15). I love this term for the local church because it gives a picture of the family that we are a part of when we become a believer. God is our father, and when we come to church, we are coming into his "house" to get to know him and spend time with our spiritual family. We are nourished, refreshed, and protected, just as we would be in a good home. And just as any good father's house is important to him, God's house is important to him as well.

The Bible tells us that Jesus is doing two things right now. First, he's seated at the right hand of the Father, praying or communicating with God on our behalf, and second, he's building his church. It's his treasure, his bride, and what Jesus gave his life for. God loves his church, and it is a significant part of his plan for humanity and for our lives personally.

No church is perfect, because the church is made up of imperfect people. But despite its imperfections, there's something powerful about an army of faithful people following and worshiping God together. What makes the church significant and powerful has little to do with a building or a style of worship. The church is God's family, and there's nothing like being surrounded by loving family relationships to support and strengthen us. In our diversity of age, race, background, and stage of life, the church is God's people coming together for one common cause—to lift up the name of Jesus and reach other people with his love. We can't replace the powerful effects of living out the gospel in a community of people who share our commitment to God.

When we struggle with people in the church, or even with the concept of church itself, we must remember why we're called to actively participate in it. It's not necessarily to make us feel good. It's to show our respect for God. We have to maintain honor in our hearts for the local church, despite the fact that there will be imperfections in it. If we take God's house for granted and view it as ordinary or unimportant, our attitude prevents us from receiving all that God wants to bring into our lives through his church.

The very thing we need—direction, encouragement, peace, comfort—may be waiting for us in God's house. When we have an attitude of respect for God's house, incredible things flow into our lives. How do we receive them? The Bible gives us the answer: "Those who are planted in the house of the LORD shall flourish in the courts of our God. They shall still bear fruit in old age; they shall be fresh and flourishing" (Ps. 92:13–14 NJKV).

We flourish and receive all the benefits of God's house when we are *planted* there! It affects our whole being—spirit, soul, and body. God's house is full of blessings, but simply visiting or popping in now and then doesn't bring the good things into our lives that God intends for us to experience. Planted means putting down roots and getting connected . . . *that's* when we flourish! There's a zest for life in our souls and our spirits instead of our being dried up and lifeless. This is the kind of abundant, overflowing life God has called us to (John 10:10). If you don't have a life-giving church where you can hear God's Word and build healthy relationships, I encourage you to find one right away and get planted.

We're called to honor God's house by doing more than just attending services or giving our finances; we need to make it a priority in our lives.

Chick-fil-A has never opened its doors on Sundays. And it's funny because I always seem to crave a juicy chicken sandwich, some waffle fries, and a mint chocolate chip milkshake on Sunday afternoons! But the decision was made long ago by Chick-fil-A's founder, Truett Cathy, a strong Christian and astute businessman. He said, "I was not so committed to financial success that I was willing to abandon my principles and priorities. One of my examples of this is our decision to close on Sunday. Our decision to close on Sunday was our way of honoring God and of directing our attention to things that matter more than our business."[1]

He made it a priority to honor the house of God so that Chick-fil-A managers and employees can go to church, rest, and worship. Today, Chick-fil-A is a 4.1-billion-dollar business with over sixteen hundred restaurants. I believe God has moved the company forward and brought momentum in a significant way because they honored him. Chick-fil-A began in a house so small that it was called the Dwarf Grill! But this dwarf has become a giant because of the way its leaders honor God and his house first.

For the Love of People

"A new command I give you: Love one another. As I have loved you, so you must love one another" (John 13:34).

Third, we honor God by honoring people. Once in a while I watch the TV show *Undercover Boss*. The owner or CEO of a corporation goes undercover and works in an entry-level position to experience firsthand how things are being handled in their company. Usually they change their appearance by growing a beard or wearing a wig so the employees won't recognize them. Sometimes I'm amazed at how some of the employees treat them. They wouldn't dream of treating the CEO of their company that way, but because they think they're just another worker, they feel like they can treat them any way they want.

It's easy to honor those we think are important, but we can be tempted to disrespect those we think are less important. Here's what we have to remember: We honor people not because of rank or status but because they are made in the image of God (Gen. 1:27). Every person inherently has value and worth because God created them. Psalm 139 says that God knew us before we were born, and he knit us together in our mother's womb. We are his masterpiece (Eph. 2:10). We honor God by honoring his workmanship—people. When we dishonor people, we dishonor God because he's the one who made them.

We can't say we love God and carry an attitude of dishonor toward people. "If anyone boasts, 'I love God,' and goes right on hating his brother or sister, thinking nothing of it, he is a liar. If he won't love the person he can see, how can he love the God he can't see? The command we have from Christ is blunt: Loving God includes loving people. You've got to love both" (1 John 4:20–21 Message).

People should matter to us because they matter more than anything to God. John 3:16 tells us, "For God so loved the world that he gave his one and only Son, that whoever believes in him shall not perish but have eternal life." In the original Greek text, the word *world* is *ethnos*, which in Greek refers to people groups. So you could say, "For God so loved people."

God gave everything—his treasured Son—for people. We didn't deserve it, but he did it anyway. We need to love and honor God, and we need to love and honor people. When we honor what matters to God, that's when we begin to get the traction we need to make progress in life.

Take a moment and allow these three ways of honoring God to soak into your heart. Pay attention to the areas of your life where God may be stirring you and asking you to change. Maybe it's honoring God by being generous in your finances, or by getting planted in God's house, or by making a change in how you see or treat certain people. When you show honor in these three areas, they will help move your life forward with momentum.

3

Honor Flows from the Heart

The human heart feels things the eyes cannot see, and knows what the mind cannot
understand.

Robert Valett

I grew up in the great state of Louisiana, a state that's unique
in many ways—New Orleans with its Mardi Gras celebra-
tions, the swamps of Acadiana with their Cajun history and
culture, rough-and-tumble oil towns like Shreveport. In Louisiana, everything is a party, bigger than life. You're likely to
hear, "*Laissez les bons temps rouler!*" which means, "Let
the good times roll!" And they do—these people know how
to have fun!

The uniqueness of the culture and the zest for life are
nowhere more prominent than in the devotion of the state's
residents to college football. For many who live there, the sun
rises and sets with their favorite team. Most of them cheer
for the Tigers of Louisiana State University, and they aren't
shy about their devotion.

At any time of year, you can spot LSU fans throughout Baton Rouge wearing shirts, hats, even pants that sport the team's purple and gold colors. During football season, you'll find them tailgating in the parking lot outside Tiger Stadium days before the game! Fans show up with their RVs, grills, big-screen televisions, and portable satellite dishes so they can watch the pregame show in the parking lot. The tailgating continues until game time, when they move inside Tiger Stadium, otherwise known as Death Valley, and scream themselves hoarse trying to motivate their team to victory. They become immersed in the passion of the moment, rooting for their beloved Tigers no matter how far behind or ahead they may be.

But don't try to argue facts with them later. Even in the midst of their crazy antics, they are taking in every detail of the game. These are people who can recall the score at the end of the third quarter from the game five years ago against Auburn. They know the quarterback's name (and whom he went on to marry from a nearby parish) from ten seasons ago. They remember every decision the referees made—good and bad.

When football season is over, they turn their attention to recruiting and following rising high school players, making note of which kids are leaning toward a rival school and which ones will make early commitments to play for the Tigers. These aren't mere fans; these are devoted followers. They don't live from the head; they live from the heart.

A Few Good Men

When Jesus went looking for disciples, there weren't any Tigers fans around at the time, but there were those who in the same way lived from the heart and had the makings of devoted followers. He didn't go to Jerusalem and conduct interviews with theology students. He didn't go through the marketplace looking for the savviest businessmen. He didn't seek out the top religious leaders.

Instead, he went to the shores of the Sea of Galilee. He sought out people who knew from experience that hard work and determination could overcome the odds, who weren't afraid of risk, and who understood the value of faithfulness and loyalty.

From what we know of the disciples, many of the twelve he chose were spontaneous, impetuous, and had an uncanny willingness to do whatever Jesus asked. They had their problems, but when asked to go in groups of two to do what Jesus had been doing—healing the sick, raising the dead, casting out evil spirits—not one of them refused. There's no record of a protest or argument about it. And when an opportunity or challenge presented itself, Peter was usually the first among them to accept it.

Peter was a tough and rugged fisherman who lived in Capernaum. He didn't have much in the way of formal education, but he had a dominant personality and was a naturally gifted leader. People wanted to be with him, and his fellow disciples were no different. According to Scripture, he was the leader and spokesman of the Twelve from the beginning and was never seriously challenged for that position. When Jesus came to the disciples in the night, walking on the water, it was Peter who asked to join him on the waves (Matt. 14:22–33).

When Moses and Elijah appeared to Jesus at the transfiguration, Peter was the one who spoke up, however awkwardly (Matt. 17:1–8). And when the guards came to arrest Jesus, it was Peter's sword that swung for the head of the high priest's slave (John 18:10).

Peter didn't write eloquent prose like John, and he didn't construct the theological arguments later offered by Paul, but if you wanted a man who volunteered first and asked about the assignment second, Peter was your man. If he'd been born in Louisiana, he would have been wearing purple and gold when Jesus found him. Peter lived from the heart.

Heart in Motion

If we are going to honor God—truly honor him in a way that produces momentum in our lives—that honor must flow from the *heart*.

At various points in history, God's people followed him, and other times they turned away from him. God used the prophet Isaiah to clearly express his thoughts on how they were treating him. "These people come near to me with their mouth and honor me with their lips, but their hearts are far from me. Their worship of me is made up only of rules taught by men" (Isa. 29:13). Basically, God says, "I don't just want your words. I don't just want your actions. I want your *hearts*."

We can be respectful and honoring with our words, but our hearts may not be in it. Praying the Lord's Prayer is more than just mouthing the words Jesus used. Anybody can say, "Our Father in heaven, I honor your name," but it's a whole different deal when we commit to living it out.

When there is a disconnect between our actions, our words, and our hearts, then we're sure to get stuck. We can continue to move forward for a while, but without a true sense of respect coming from our hearts, our actions become lifeless habits. We're just going through the motions. It's kind of like riding those stationary bikes at the gym. Yes, we're on a bike and we're pedaling, but we're not going anywhere. The heart is a necessary, vital component. It has to be engaged.

Cross Your Heart

When you were a kid, did you ever make a pact with a friend and seal it with "cross your heart, hope to die"? Even then we were acknowledging the vital role our hearts play in how we commit to someone, in how we tell the truth, and in how we live our lives. That catchy phrase is easy to say but more difficult to live out.

We can fall into the same trap. I talk to a lot of people, and often they're doing and saying the "right" things, but their hearts aren't fully engaged. I think that's why so many people find church or a relationship with God dry, unsatisfying, and uninteresting.

Jesus came to make a passionate, vibrant relationship with the Father possible for you and me. This can happen only when our hearts are "all in" with God. He isn't looking for halfhearted lip service or empty adherence to a set of rules and regulations. Here's the key: *True* honor flows from the heart.

I'm not saying that the mind is unimportant or that we don't need good, solid theology. We can't just do whatever we want and say, "God understands—he knows my heart." That's not it at all. However, having high regard for God means so much more than following a list of do's and don'ts.

When a religious expert of the law asked Jesus to name the most important commandment, Jesus pointed him back to the heart. "'Love the Lord your God with all your heart and with all your soul and with all your mind.' This is the first and greatest commandment" (Matt. 22:37–38).

The Pharisees were all about the "do"—what they could or couldn't do, the external appearance of making sure they had the reputation of being righteous. Jesus rocked their world when he took them back to the heart! The soul and mind were important, but when Jesus answered them, the heart came first. The Message puts it this way: "Love the Lord your God with all your passion." I'm talking about honor with passionate enthusiasm. Peter's kind of honor! An LSU Tigers fan's kind of honor!

Passion in Practice

Passion and honor are intimately connected. The best example is the life of Jesus. His respect and reverence for his Father produced such great passion that he willingly gave his life for the people his Father loved. Honor should produce intensity and zeal in our lives that move us to action, even if it's difficult. When passion and honor coexist, sooner or later forward momentum is going to take place.

I know that not everyone's personality is the same, so passion may not always produce spontaneous, combustible, explosive living the way it does in some people like Peter. I tend to have a little of that in me too, but my wife, Leslie, in some ways is just the opposite of me. She is careful and counts the cost much more than I do. She is thorough and more reserved. But she is a passionate person. Her life is full of conviction and commitment to what she believes, and she is constantly pressing ahead as a result of the passion in her heart.

Honor and passion are less about our personality types and more about giving God a place of genuine awe and respect in our hearts. When God is at the center, he impacts the way we live our lives.

There is so much in the Bible about the heart, but there are two verses I want to highlight. Proverbs 23:7 says, "For as he thinks in his heart, so is he" (AMP), and Proverbs 4:23 gives us this instruction: "Guard your heart above all else, for it determines the course of your life" (NLT).

Two keys emerge from the heart's role in honoring God. First, the real test of who we are is what's in our hearts. Our heart's attitude determines who we are and whom we will become. Second, our hearts determine where we go in life, the path we walk, and our final destination. No wonder then that the Bible tells us to guard our hearts "above all else"— the heart is one of the most significant treasures to protect.

Heart Conditions

If we fail to honor from our hearts, we create roadblocks on our path to progress. Let's think about some "heart conditions" that can prevent genuine honor from flowing from the core of who we are.

First is the hard heart, or what I would call the stubborn heart. The stubborn heart says, "I'm going to get my way or do it my way no matter what. I don't care what it takes or what the consequences are. It's my way or the highway."

In Exodus 7 and 8, we read that Pharaoh had a hard heart. He had several opportunities to stop the plagues God was sending Egypt, but he wouldn't budge. That stubborn heart led to a headstrong stance that resulted in tremendous loss and tragedy in his life and in his nation. He failed to realize that you can never win a battle of wills when you're set against God.

It's good to have a strong will toward the right things, but it can be dangerous too and can keep us from God's best if we don't manage it carefully. We can hold too tightly to what we think is best instead of submitting to God and acknowledging that his plans and purposes are better. A hard heart won't honor because it's already determined how things should be. It's frozen and immovable. A soft and willing heart, on the other hand, can trust that God's way is the best way and can honor him, even when it doesn't know or understand everything. We must remain soft and flexible.

Another heart condition is the proud heart. It says, "I don't need God or anyone else; I can take care of this on my own." It has a difficult time giving respect, whether it's to God or to other people. But the Bible says, "God opposes the proud but gives grace to the humble" (1 Peter 5:5). Pride is one of the biggest reasons we struggle to honor. Pride causes resistance from God, and it usually creates resistance from people as well. You may think you're better than someone else and they don't really deserve your honor. I encourage you to make a 180-degree turn and be quick to honor, freely and easily. Stop calculating whether you think they've earned it. Pride builds roadblocks to progress in life. Don't let it keep you from the benefits honor can bring. A humble heart has a powerful impact not only in our walk with God but also in our relationships with others.

Sometimes we experience a hurt that makes it difficult to trust or to give honor, especially when the hurt was caused by someone in authority over us. Someone with an injured or wounded heart often struggles because someone in authority misused them or let them down. For example, if you had a difficult relationship with your earthly mom or dad, it may be hard for you to honor God or people in a position of authority over you. No matter what relationship caused you this pain, you have to allow God to bring healing and restoration so that you can release honor and respect the way he wants you to.

A skeptical or distrusting heart refuses to believe in the best or hope for happiness. It may even scoff at honor as naïve and foolhardy. We may have a fearful heart, a doubting heart, a faint heart (one that can't withstand challenges or hard times), or a half-committed heart. Usually these heart conditions all boil down to being unable to trust God and surrender our wills and our lives to him. We can't—or won't—honor him if we don't trust him and believe he has our best interest in mind. If he has only a part of us, then he doesn't have all of us. And if he doesn't have all of us, then we're not honoring him fully.

Straight from the Heart

Has your heart checked out for some reason? Are you just going through the motions? Sometimes this happens, and we don't even realize it. If there is an area in which you've let your heart slip out of gear and it's not fully engaged, I encourage you to take some steps to get your heart back in alignment with God.

To regain a healthy heart, you'll have to invest some effort in working through the things that can block honor from flowing out. Take some time to do an honest evaluation regarding the condition of your heart. If you have a heart condition, humble yourself enough to admit you're wrong and ask God to forgive you. Then make a commitment to change the perspectives and attitudes that led to that heart condition. Just like a healthy heart in a physical body requires a good diet and exercise, a spiritual heart does too. Search God's Word for the specific truths that will help you strengthen your heart in the area you may need to change. As you take in Scripture and put it into action, you are providing a healthy diet and exercise for your spiritual heart.

More than anything, God wants our hearts. He doesn't want honor to be reduced to the words rolling off our lips. He wants it to be something that comes from deep within. True honor flows straight from the heart.

4

Honor Opens Doors

Honor is better than honors.

Abraham Lincoln

My wife, Leslie, comes from a large Italian family. We've been married for over twenty years now, and during this time, I've loved being a part of the family and getting to experience a little bit of the Italian culture through Leslie's relatives. Not only did I gain an amazing wife, but I've also been able to enjoy a lot of great Italian food and many lively family gatherings. But another thing that has impacted me greatly is my relationship with Leslie's dad. From the start, and still today, talking with Leslie's dad is one of my favorite things to do when I'm with her family.

Since he's Italian, I like to joke with him and throw out lines from the movie *The Godfather* and ask questions about the mafia. But the truth is, my father-in-law is an honest, hardworking man and is the furthest thing from a mafia godfather. He does agree with Don Vito Corleone though when he says, "There's nothing more important to a man than his family."

It's how he was raised and it's the Italian way. In their culture, elders are highly respected and honored, even in the little things. When he was growing up, family time at the dinner table was a big deal. His dad, the patriarch, was always served first. After that, everyone else was served in order of age. Being the youngest of twelve kids in their family, Leslie's dad was always served last. By the time the serving plate got to him, all that was left was the neck of the chicken. To this day, it's still his favorite part!

Leslie's dad was a successful businessman and led a thriving division of a large corporation. He's very smart and lives out his faith with godly character. While he's never led a church or started a ministry, I've gained a lot of wisdom and counsel from him over the years that have helped me in pastoring and leading a church. Since he's never really done what I do, I could have dismissed his input about how I should manage and operate a church.

If I had done that, I would have done myself a serious disservice. But because I honored him, a door opened between us, and I was able to gain valuable perspective and the wisdom his decades of experience brought him. The incredible wealth of knowledge he had gained from his years of leading a corporation, working with people, and operating in the business world flowed into my life, and I was able to receive the benefits. I've learned many key business principles, from cultivating growth to managing people, and he has offered insight on many specific decisions along the way.

Greater still, his influence in my life impacted me personally, and it has increased my capacity and skill as a leader and an administrator. Without him even knowing it, God used him in my life to lead me forward. Honor opens doors.

The X Factor

I like to say that honor is a gateway virtue: It opens up paths of opportunity and leads us into better things. I'm convinced that honor is often the X factor in the equation—the variable that determines the final outcome. The amount of honor we give something determines the benefit we will be able to receive from it. If we choose to honor something—a particular opportunity, situation, or person, even the difficult ones—we will be able to extract all the value that it holds. But if we withhold honor from something, we miss out on all that it could bring into our lives. Just as this was true in my relationship with Leslie's dad, it's true in our relationship with God too.

To hallow or to honor is to respect something greatly—to hold it in high regard. To dishonor something means that we treat it as common or ordinary, as if there's nothing special about it. There's a clear example of this in the Bible.

Jesus was from a town called Nazareth, and on one occasion he was teaching in the synagogue there. Jesus received various kinds of responses in the different places he went. Some loved him, some hated him, some were intrigued by him.

But in Nazareth, his hometown, the people were offended by him. We're told they "disapproved of Him, and it hindered them from acknowledging His authority" (Matt. 6:3 AMP). I imagine they murmured, "Who does he think he is?" Because they were familiar with him, they saw him as common and ordinary. And the way they saw him determined what they received from him.

In response, Jesus said, "'Only in his hometown, among his relatives and in his own house is a prophet without honor.' He could not do any miracles there, except lay his hands on a few sick people and heal them. And he was amazed at their lack of faith" (Mark 6:4–6). They failed to receive all God had for them because of their lack of honor. Their disrespect and dishonor kept them from receiving all he came to bring them. They closed the door that honor provided instead of walking through it.

Chain Reaction

So many times there's value, benefit, and blessing locked up in something, just waiting to be released. It makes me think of junior high science experiments about energy and chemical reactions. Potential energy is locked up in individual ingredients, but it needs a reagent—a specific ingredient added to get the reaction going—to be released. It's similar to a catalyst, but while a catalyst is something that speeds up a reaction, a reagent is something that initiates a reaction—it's what gets the whole process started. When you add a reagent to the test tube, it sets off a chain reaction. The mixture starts bubbling and smoking and popping, and the test tube overflows.

Honor is a "reagent" in our lives. It's the ingredient that will unleash the benefits within the people and situations God has placed in our lives. Are there people or situations in your life right now that you should honor more? There may be some incredible things waiting on the other side of honor that could impact you in a significant way.

Don't make the mistake of seeing things as ordinary when you should see them as extraordinary. Look for the extraordinary in people through the eyes of honor and you will position yourself to receive all that God wants to bring into your life through them.

Jesus wanted to do so much more for the people of Nazareth, but he couldn't. Notice that the Bible doesn't say he *would not* do any miracles. It says he *could not*. Dishonor closed the door on their opportunity to receive from God.

However, the opposite is also true. God responds when we honor him. Honor opens the door, and on the other side of the door rewards are waiting. Two of those rewards are knowledge and wisdom. We're told, "The fear of the LORD is the beginning of knowledge, but fools despise wisdom and instruction" (Prov. 1:7). The fear of the Lord isn't about being scared of God; it's about having reverent respect for him.

Whether it's a relationship, a work situation, issues with a spouse, problems with our children, struggles with our attitude, or clarity about the next step we should take, God's Word gives us what we need to navigate anything we may face in life. But if we ignore its wisdom or dismiss its principles as old-fashioned or not culturally relevant, then we forgo all the potential power it has to transform our lives. Respect for God and his Word, the Bible, opens the door to the amazing knowledge and divine wisdom that can strengthen every area of our lives.

Honoring Others

Some of the greatest rewards of honor come when it's applied within the context of our everyday relationships. Jesus said, "He who receives you receives me, and he who receives me receives the one who sent me. Anyone who receives a prophet because he is a prophet will receive a prophet's reward, and anyone who receives a righteous man because he is a righteous man will receive a righteous man's reward. And if anyone gives even a cup of cold water to one of these little ones because he is my disciple, I tell you the truth, he will certainly not lose his reward" (Matt. 10:40–44).

Jesus identifies three levels of relationship that require honor: people in authority over us, those who are alongside us, and those who are below us.

Authority Figures

Romans 13:1 tells us that all authority comes from God, so we must respect the position of those in authority over us as well as who they are as people. Paul is talking about all kinds of leadership figures here—bosses, parents, government officials, police officers, teachers, coaches—anyone in authority over us.

In fact, the only one of the Ten Commandments that has a reward attached to it is the one that has to do with honor and authority. Paul refers to it in Ephesians 6:2–3, saying, "'Honor your father and mother'—which is the first commandment with a promise—'that it may go well with you and that you may enjoy long life on the earth.'"

Keep in mind that just because every authority has been given by God does not mean that every authority is godly. But even if someone is acting in an ungodly way, our job is to have an attitude of respect toward them. When we do, a reward flows into our lives. Please understand that I'm not talking about being mistreated or abused. I'm talking about having to treat those above us better than they are sometimes treating us.

Authority is an issue for many people. If you have issues with authority, you're going to have a hard time keeping a job, maintaining health in relationships, or making progress in general. If you're someone who always wants to resist authority and go in the opposite direction, try saying yes and being accommodating. Honor flows out of a humble heart, and James 4:6 tells us that God shows favor to the humble. Not only does God's favor flow toward us when we show respect and honor to those above us, it naturally creates favor with the person we are treating with respect and honor.

People in authority aren't perfect, but a reward will come into your life just by honoring them and the authority God has given them because that's what God asks you to do.

Meeting Your Match

Jesus also shows us that we must extend respect to those alongside us—friends, peers, those we work with. This area is often the hardest because we are at an equal, and sometimes competitive, level. We come alongside these people and feel we need to one-up them.

Instead, we must look for opportunities to show them honor. Next time your co-worker says, "Hey! Will you do me a favor? Will you make some copies for me? I need them for our meeting after lunch, but I have an appointment I need to get to," instead of saying, "No, because last time I checked you're not my boss," why don't you try a different approach and help them? Be willing to go the extra mile. Maybe even exceed their expectations by running to the copy place around the block and making color copies for them.

Why not? When you live this way, honor will set you apart and cause you to stand out. The next time the boss goes down the list for promotions and bonuses, your name may just be on the top of the list because you have the reputation of working well with people and respecting them.

Our words, our actions, our attitudes, even our body language are all areas we can check when we ask ourselves, "How can I show more honor to those around me?" Whether it's a friend, a co-worker, or a spouse, a little honor goes a long way and can make a big difference.

The Honor Roll

Finally, Jesus tells us to treat those below us with honor as well. He says, "And if you give even a cup of cold water to one of the least of my followers, you will surely be rewarded" (Matt. 10:42 NLT). By below, I don't mean that anyone's value is beneath that of another person. People below us are the people we have authority over, carry responsibility for, or have leadership over. These people are our children, the people who work for us, the people on a team we lead, or people who do things for us—for example, people who serve us at restaurants, make repairs, or help us at a store.

The people who wait on us in a restaurant are just as important as we are, and we have an obligation to honor them and be respectful. I've seen people treat waiters and waitresses poorly simply because they could, even when the servers were doing a good job.

Just because we're in a position of authority doesn't mean we should take advantage of it or act like a dictator. Jesus himself said that he "did not come to be served, but to serve" (Matt. 20:28). His example is the ultimate leadership model. We need to be careful with the authority God gives us because he won't give us any more if he can't trust us with what he has already given. When we respect people who are entrusted into our authority and care, we have an opportunity to be a reflection of Jesus, and it usually opens the door for us to have greater influence in their lives. We must value them and see them as God sees them.

The Road Less Traveled

Choosing to live with honor will distinguish you and cause you to stand out among the crowd. It will open doors of favor and opportunity. Decide to be the person who lives with honor—even if no one else in your world does.

I love Robert Frost's poem "The Road Not Taken," especially the final three lines:

> Two roads diverged in a wood, and I—
> I took the one less traveled by,
> And that has made all the difference.[1]

The path of honor is the less-traveled road. But it is the path that will lead you forward into true significance. Choose to live a life of extraordinary honor and watch God open doors in your life. It may not happen overnight, but you can be sure that God honors those who honor him. When you treat the people in your world well, you are honoring God, and that will always pay off in the end.

I encourage you to pray this prayer as you reflect on what you've learned about honor.

One step forward: My Father in heaven, hallowed be your name. I honor you, and I want that honor to flow from my heart and be evident in every area of my life. I want my life to be marked by honor in my relationship with you, in how I handle myself, and in how I treat others—whether they are in authority over me, work alongside me, or travel behind me. I want to walk through every open door that honor unlocks and be able to receive the rewards that come in response to honor. May I honor you, God, now and forever. In Jesus's name, amen.

RENEWAL

ALLOWING GOD TO CHANGE YOU
FROM THE INSIDE OUT

5

Your Kingdom Come

> Your kingdom come, your will be done on
> earth as it is in heaven.
>
> Matthew 6:10

As we have seen in our exploration of the Lord's Prayer, the first thing Jesus did in coming to his Father was to offer honor. The very next thing he did was to align himself with the plans and purposes of the Father. He made the choice to acknowledge his Father's authority and will above his own. In essence, he said, "Father, have your way . . ." This is a key for us too as we come to our Father. This may be one of the most difficult things for us as human beings to do—to truly submit our will and acknowledge the will of God as supreme, choosing it above all else. But it is also one of the most powerful things we can do if we want to have God-given momentum in our lives.

In his book *The Great Divorce*, C. S. Lewis said, "There are only two kinds of people in the end: those who say to

God, 'Thy will be done,' and those to whom God says, in the end, 'Thy will be done.'"[1] God won't force his will on us, but acknowledging it above ours and embracing it puts us in the best possible place for our lives to succeed on God's terms—which is the only true form of success.

To unlock the power of this second part of the Lord's Prayer, we need to understand what Jesus was doing when he prayed this. When we pray, "Your kingdom come, your will be done on earth as it is in heaven," we are asking that God's ways, his authority, his priorities, his purpose, his plans, and all the benefits of heaven would operate here on earth, just as they do there. In heaven, we will trade the heartache and pain we experience on earth for a life of joy. We will exchange a world full of sin and corruption for unimaginable beauty and peace. Even sickness and death are left behind for eternal wholeness and healing.

We aren't there now, but Jesus told us to pray that God's way of doing things would become established on earth. When we seek for his will to be done on earth, this desire affects the primary focus and priorities of our lives. It changes us from the inside out.

C. S. Lewis may be best known for writing the beloved Chronicles of Narnia, but he also wrote many books that stemmed from his faith journey. He is an incredible example of someone whose life was completely changed by an understanding of God. God used books Lewis read and his Christian friends to work on his heart. Lewis went from being an atheist to one of the most well-known defenders of the Christian faith, giving talks and writing books that have helped countless people understand and embrace Christianity. He knew the power of having a kingdom-minded perspective. He said, "If you read history you will find that the Christians who did most for the present world were precisely those who thought most of the next."[2] When we are focused on God's kingdom and we live our days on earth with an eternal, heaven-focused mind-set, we are transformed. I call this renewal.

Recipe for Renewal

When we begin to follow Jesus's pattern and take on a "your will be done" approach to life and our relationship with God, we experience some amazing benefits. First, renewal brings transformation. Renewal changes us from the inside out so that we begin to look completely different. This is the principle we learn from the second part of the Lord's Prayer. This kind of renewal requires us to give everything we are and everything we have to God. This is how Paul explains it in Romans 12:1: "So here's what I want you to do, God helping you: Take your everyday, ordinary life—your sleeping, eating, going-to-work, and walking-around life—and place it before God as an offering. Embracing what God does for you is the best thing you can do for him" (Message). Romans 12:2 gives us further encouragement, saying, "Do not conform any longer to the pattern of this world, but be transformed by the renewing of your mind. Then you will be able to test and approve what God's will is—his good, pleasing and perfect will."

The word used for transformation is *metamorpho*, from which we get our word *metamorphosis*, which means "to become completely new and different." Think about a caterpillar folding itself into a little cocoon and then emerging as a spectacularly beautiful butterfly. That's metamorphosis!

The new you that comes out of this process is stronger and has greater capacity to take on more and accomplish more. You don't settle for mediocre and middle of the road. You take the high road, the road less traveled, and pursue excellence according to God's standards, not the standards of others. The new you is not defined by what other people think about you. The new you is stronger, wiser, and more equipped to move ahead into God's plan for your life.

We can so easily become attached to our own ways of doing things that we forget about God's ways. We can get so immersed in *our* agendas, *our* ideas, *our* visions, *our* desires that we forget to say, "*Your* kingdom come, *your* will be done." Renewal is the solution. We have to let go of our ways of doing things and take on God's way of doing things.

The connection between renewal and momentum is a powerful one. For some people, the greatest obstacle to getting unstuck and beginning to make progress in life is their unwillingness to change. A new thought, a new habit, a new perspective could revolutionize their present and jump-start their future, but so many times they find it difficult to change and do things a different way.

If we are willing to embrace change and trust that God's heavenly plans and purposes are best, we'll find that we can experience the transformation promised in Romans 12:2—the kind of transformation that leaves us completely new and different, the kind of transformation that changes us to be more like Jesus and to see his kingdom come on earth and in our personal lives. The men who were closest to Jesus, his disciples, knew this kind of metamorphosis firsthand. "They preached with joyful urgency that life can be *radically different*" (Mark 6:12 Message, emphasis mine).

No matter what your life looks like right now, the power of God is able to bring change and transformation to any area of your life that needs renewal.

Vital Connection

Second, renewal keeps us connected to God's will, or his plan for our lives. This is what we're asking for when we pray, "Your kingdom come, your will be done." Almost all of us would say that we want to know God's plan for our lives. Even people who don't consider themselves religious cry out to God at times when they are searching for their purpose in life or when they are faced with the weight of making a life-changing decision. We are wired with a God-given desire to have purpose and a plan for our lives.

When we allow God to renew us, we can then "test and approve what God's will is—his good, pleasing and perfect will" (Rom. 12:2). Our way of doing things has serious limitations. We can't see the future, and we often can't see how certain events and relationships work in tandem to bring about God's will. Our own thoughts, experiences, and perspectives tend to color things and get in the way. So we must rely on him and trust him fully.

As we constantly allow ourselves to be changed by God, it's like we are adjusting and course correcting a little bit each step along our journey. We avoid the distractions and detours that can come if we try to hang on to our old ways of thinking and doing things.

Global Expansion

Third, renewal enlarges our world, both inside and out. Have you ever noticed how much bigger your life feels after you return home from a trip, especially if the trip took you to a place radically different from your own? Leslie and I certainly experienced this sense of global expansion when we moved to Kenya to serve a church there.

During our time in Africa, Leslie and I had the opportunity to see some of the most breathtaking scenery you can imagine: the expansive beauty of the Serengeti with its endless plains of tall green grasses, acacia trees, and exotic animals, the way the blue sky stretched across the entire horizon. The culture there was very different as well. We had to learn new customs, new ways of accomplishing basic tasks such as shopping and cooking, not to mention new languages.

When we allow God to renew us, he clears out the old and makes room for all the new and good things he wants to bring into our lives. We gain a larger perspective and maybe even a larger vision for our life and future. It opens up possibilities we didn't see before. Renewal is challenging sometimes because it means change and adjustment on our part. Leslie and I had to press through the discomfort of learning a new routine and way of doing things in Africa. Living in a place that was so different from what we were used to was tough at times, but it expanded our way of thinking, added new skills to our lives, and enlarged our hearts in a powerful way as we learned to love and appreciate a beautiful new people and their way of life.

The Bible describes this process as having tailored clothes that are always being altered to fit us as we grow. "And have clothed yourselves with the new [spiritual self], which is [ever in the process of being] renewed and remolded into [fuller and more perfect knowledge upon] knowledge after the image (the likeness) of Him Who created it" (Col. 3:10 AMP).

Child's Play

Finally, renewal keeps us youthful and full of life. Our culture definitely places an emphasis on youth and a desire to remain energetic and attractive, but I'm not talking about that. What I'm referring to is having a youthful quality deep within, a zest for life that pours out of our spirit and soul. As the psalmist writes, we worship a God "who satisfies your desires with good things so that your youth is renewed like the eagle's" (Ps. 103:5).

Having a youthful spirit means we're full of joy, curious about life, and full of gratitude and appreciation for all of creation. A youthful spirit is not determined by age—in fact, I've met some people in their eighties who are more youthful than some teenagers!

Renewal keeps us from becoming stagnant. It prevents us from growing bitter, cynical, or disheartened. We know our purpose through God's will and find joy in being all he created us to be. This quality of youthfulness expresses itself through our energy, our willingness to change, our innocence, and our drive to initiate change.

Have you ever watched little kids at play? They're so carefree and aren't trying to have everything in life figured out. One of the key characteristics of youthfulness is an excitement about each day. Sometimes life's trials and disappointments can cause us to lose this quality as adults. Jesus told us we must come to God as little children if we want to enter into the kingdom of heaven. We must cultivate childlike faith and wonder, a sense of trust and devotion.

Renewal is a powerful force that can drastically change our lives for the better. But what we have to remember is that renewal is a daily and ongoing process, not something that takes place once in a while or is completed all at once. We can't give up if we aren't instantly changed into what we think we should be. "Therefore we do not lose heart. Though outwardly we are wasting away, yet inwardly we are being renewed day by day" (2 Cor. 4:16).

A major key to dynamic forward momentum is spiritual renewal, getting rid of the old (our way of doing things) and embracing the new (God's way of doing things). Don't walk into your future clinging to yesterday's mind-sets. Renewal will transform you and prepare you for all God has for you as you allow him to work in your life, re-creating you from the inside out.

6

Make Up Your Mind

You are what you are and where you are
because of what has gone into your mind.
You can change what you are and where you
are by changing what goes into your mind.

Zig Ziglar

As children in science class, we learned that the mind is what controls our ability to move, to see, and to perform every other bodily function. But the mind is more than just a processing center that helps our bodies operate properly. Our attitudes, mental outlooks, and expectations impact every area of our lives, and these are all controlled by our minds. Our minds take in data from the world around us, process thoughts, form feelings, and help us take action.

Scripture reveals that the mind is connected to the heart, which is where our deepest thoughts and feelings reside: "As he thinks in his heart, so is he" (Prov. 23:7 NKJV). What we think defines and creates us. It determines who we are and what we become. Whatever we believe to be true determines what actions we take.

If you're all alone walking down a dark, unfamiliar city street late at night, you might expect a person you meet to be a mugger, even though he might actually be a tourist, someone getting off work, or even a police officer. Because of the setting and whatever associations you've formed based on the news accounts you've read or the movies you've seen, you view the environment as dangerous, whether it is or not. Or consider a more basic example. You can say you're not afraid to fly, but if you refuse to ride in a plane, then the truth is you really are afraid to fly.

There's no doubt about it. Our minds and hearts contain the potential to unlock our destinies or destroy them. What we think can either catapult us forward toward all that God has for us or drag us backward into old habits, where we get stuck in place. I love how clearly the New Living Translation puts it: "Let God transform you by changing the way you think" (Rom. 12:2).

The starting point for true change is found as we renew our minds, replacing our thoughts with God's thoughts. As we take on this pursuit of renewal that Jesus modeled for us by praying, "Your kingdom come, your will be done on earth as it is in heaven," it brings change to our minds and, as a result, to the rest of our lives.

Ephesians 4:23 gives us this encouragement: "And be constantly renewed in the spirit of your mind [having a fresh mental and spiritual attitude]" (AMP). We may be able to accomplish a certain amount of change on our own, but we need God's renewing power to bring true, lasting transformation.

Think Twice

Researchers estimate that we have up to sixty thousand thoughts per day—and as many as 98 percent of them are exactly the same as we had the day before! And the vast majority of these thoughts, as much as 80 percent, tend to be negative.[1]

Most of us have heard this definition of insanity: "Doing the same thing over and over again and expecting different results." What many of us don't realize is that we keep *doing* the same things because we are *thinking* the same things. We need to start thinking twice about what we think. Wrong thinking can slow us down, keep us stuck, or even completely derail our lives. I have seen people's lives ruined by what was taking place in their minds and thoughts. Something small that starts in our minds can eventually lead us down some bad roads in life.

Over the years, I have had to change or improve certain ways of thinking. When Leslie and I were first married, we had a lot of debt. I didn't know much at all about how to manage finances. The way I grew up, if you wanted something, you bought it. If you couldn't afford to pay for it with cash, you just put it on a credit card. I had no concept of budgeting—in fact, I'm not sure I had even heard the word *budget* until I was in college. That concept was the furthest thing from my mind when it came to money.

To me, credit cards gave me the "freedom" I wanted in my finances. But no one told me how quickly those charges add up and how deadly the interest rates are. Our finances were a mess. Finally, I got fed up with being in debt, and we worked hard to pay it off. It was pretty incredible, considering how much debt we had. But then I slipped back into my old ways of doing things, and before I knew it, we were right back in debt again, this time worse than before.

I knew something had to change, so I prayed that God would get us out of debt. But he didn't. Nothing changed overnight like I had hoped. Then I started looking at finances from God's perspective and learning what he had to say about money, and as I did, my mind changed. And as my mind changed, I began making better choices. Those better choices eventually turned into better habits, and better habits helped us get out of debt . . . and stay out of debt.

I wanted God to change the problem, but he wanted to change me by renewing my mind. Renewal took place as I started identifying the emotions and thoughts I had associated with money, credit, and debt.

Toxic Thoughts

I've discovered that a variety of emotionally charged issues contribute to flawed thinking patterns and negative mind-sets. Just as an open wound can get infected, our emotional injuries can leave us susceptible to toxic thoughts. We must identify the different toxins that can infect our thinking if we want to enjoy a healthy mind.

One of them is negativity. This is a big one for many people. Some people are just naturally critical and seem bent toward a negative attitude. No matter what happens, they always expect the worst. And then they wonder why only negative things happen to them! I've found that we often get what we expect.

Fear is another issue that causes many people to live beneath God's best. As God tells us in his Word, "God has not given us a spirit of fear, but of power and of love and of a sound mind" (2 Tim. 1:7 NKJV). Fear can hold us back and keep us from stepping toward God and moving toward something new. When we're afraid, we tend to hang back. Our fear keeps us from being bold, holds us in indecision, and ultimately immobilizes us. If we let it, our fear keeps us from knowing who we are in Christ and believing in the plans and purpose God has for us.

One of the issues that can become the most toxic is insecurity because it attacks the very core of who we are and our worth and value. When we fail to base our identity on the truth of God's Word, we open ourselves up to attacks by the enemy. The devil tries to assault our identity and distort how we think about ourselves and how we think about God.

When God Changes Our Minds

We must learn to see ourselves as God sees us and believe what he says about us rather than what others say or even what we feel to be true about ourselves. He says that we are chosen, significant, created for a purpose, uniquely gifted, and beautiful. We are overcomers and champions, his victors and not the enemy's victims. When we start to believe what God says about us, our lives will change. We will begin to walk forward in our purpose, heads held high, knowing we are loved and have worth because that's what our Creator says.

Many people are robbed of joy and wholeness in life because of life-controlling issues such as substance abuse, depression, sexual addiction, eating disorders, self-harm, and many others. These behaviors are largely influenced by what takes place in their hearts and minds. If we want to live a life of freedom, we've got to take inventory of what's taking place in our minds.

Faulty thinking is going to slow us down and will most likely affect our quality of life and how much success we enjoy. Sometimes we don't even realize that faulty thinking is causing problems in our lives. Or maybe we do realize it, but we struggle to make changes.

That's where the principle of renewal becomes so powerful. We have to allow God to bring new, fresh ways of thinking into our minds. We have to renew our minds by getting rid of the lies and replacing them with the truth if we want to move forward in life.

No matter how strong the hold of wrong thinking is, there is a power that's greater: God's power. God can set us free in our minds. We have to stop thinking about the wrong things and start thinking about the right things. We need to fill our minds so full of the truth that there's no room for the lies—the poor thinking that's holding us back. "And now, dear brothers and sisters, one final thing. Fix your thoughts on what is true, and honorable, and right, and pure, and lovely, and admirable. Think about things that are excellent and worthy of praise" (Phil. 4:8 NLT).

According to the world-renowned Mayo Clinic, positive thinking produces numerous health benefits, including lower rates of depression, increased life span, lower levels of stress, stronger immune systems (and greater resistance to the common cold), reduced risk of death from cardiovascular disease, and better coping skills for difficult circumstances.[2]

Every area of our life benefits when we have positive, healthy thoughts that are based in the truth of God's Word. But, to receive those benefits, we have to put in the effort to discipline our minds and retrain our thought patterns. You *can* become a positive person. Depression, disappointment, addiction, insecurity, and fear don't have to rule you. They can be replaced with joy, hope, freedom, and confidence. God wants you to have peace and wholeness in your mind. He can change your life from the inside out if you will follow what he tells you to do.

Angry Birds

Transformation takes place as we renew our minds, and God's Word is the key to this. The Bible has the power to change us because it's the ultimate source of truth, and truth is what sets us free (John 8:32).

Did you know that when you develop thinking patterns they literally wear a path in your brain to make it easier and faster for those thoughts to travel through your brain? That's why it can be so hard to change our thought patterns—they are literally engrained in our minds. To create a new thought, we have to wear a new pathway into our mind to bypass the old one. It takes several weeks for a new path to develop, which is why it takes time to break old habits and develop new ones.[3]

Richard Davidson, neuroscientist and researcher at the University of Wisconsin, states that their research discovered positive changes in the mind of a person who meditates compared to someone who does not.[4] This is fascinating because the Bible actually instructs us to meditate on God's Word (Josh. 1:8 NLT). Doing this helps us discover the truth about God, what he says about us, and his plan for our lives and how we should live (Rom. 12:2). Studying God's Word has the power to keep us on track and following the right path (Ps. 119:9–16). It has a cleansing effect (Eph. 5:26) and strengthens our faith (Rom. 10:17).

So many times we focus on the behaviors or the issues in our lives that we want to change or get rid of. But if we don't address the thinking behind them, we're really just addressing the symptoms, not the cause, and those issues or behaviors will keep popping back up. Lasting change comes when we push down to the root of the issue and change our thinking. God wants to change us, not just our behaviors or situations. The real miracle of renewal is being able to live in sustained freedom as God changes our minds.

One of the keys to transforming our minds is learning how to filter our thoughts. We must identify poor thinking and then replace it with good thinking that's based in truth. Just because a thought comes into our hearts and minds doesn't make it true or right. It doesn't mean we have to dwell on it or allow it to stay. Martin Luther likened our thoughts to birds flying overhead. He said that we can't stop birds from flying over our heads, but we can keep them from building a nest in our hair! Kind of gives a new meaning to "angry birds"!

Food for Thought

Some people just go with whatever thoughts come into their heads, and these thoughts often get them in trouble. The truth is that *we* get to choose what we allow to stay in our hearts and minds. We can—and must—reject thoughts that don't line up with God's Word. Paul tells us that we are to take captive every thought that doesn't line up with the knowledge of God and make it obedient to Christ (2 Cor. 10:4–5).

Here are some practical ways to change your mind, literally. First, become more aware of what's going on in your thought life. Identify the poor thinking that may be lurking in your mind and causing problems in your life. What specific things trip you up? What part of your thinking doesn't line up with God's Word? Are there labels on your life that you need to get rid of?

Next, replace toxic thoughts with good, life-giving, momentum-building thoughts. Go to a church where you can hear God's Word taught in a clear way. Read the Bible on your own and study it. Get a notebook and write down thoughts as you read. If there's an issue in your life that needs changing, find Scripture passages that deal with that topic. Write them on a card and tape it on your bathroom mirror so you can memorize them.

It's also crucial that you watch what you take in. You may need to adjust what you're listening to on the radio, looking at online, reading, watching on TV, or receiving from the people who speak into your life—friends, co-workers, and even family. Practical habits such as these will allow you to kick the transformation process into high gear.

Finally, stay committed to the process. You can't renew your mind on your own. When you try to change your mind through sheer determination and willpower, you end up frustrated and failing. But when you invite God's power into your will, then you have a whole new power source. If you truly desire God's kingdom to come and you seek it as your primary focus, your life can't help but be changed. Renewing your mind usually doesn't happen overnight, but it does happen, one thought at a time, as you pursue God's kingdom and his will. Slowly your actions become more like his and your thoughts become closer to his. Allow God's renewing power to change your mind and it will change your life.

7

Carpe Momentum

You can clutch the past so tightly to your
chest that it leaves your arms too full to embrace the present.

Jan Glidewell

Have you ever known someone who was living in a moment
of achievement from decades ago? You know who I'm talking
about. You meet a guy who says, "Well, back in '81 when we
took the state title . . ." Then you go to his house and there's
a shrine to his high school football achievements. You want
to say, "That was awesome—but that was thirty years ago.
Face it. You aren't in high school anymore. Time to let it go
and move on. Stop living in the past!" His glory days have
turned into a glory daze!

As a pastor, I've found that one of the reasons people can't
move forward in life is that they're stuck in a moment from
their past. U2's song "Stuck in a Moment" sums up many
of these situations well: "You've got stuck in a moment, and
you can't get out of it."

The second we stop moving and linger a moment longer than we should, we are setting ourselves up to get stuck. God reminds us of the importance of looking forward rather than backward in Isaiah 43:18–19: "Forget the former things; do not dwell on the past. See, I am doing a new thing! Now it springs up; do you not perceive it? I am making a way in the desert and streams in the wasteland."

If we want God's kingdom to come and his will to be done, then we have to let go of the old to make room for new things to take root and be established. God wants to renew us, but if we are lost in the past and refuse to let it go, we drastically reduce the amount of renewal that can take place. Many times people want to change, but often God does the most significant renewing work when they take the initiative to let go of the past and take the first step toward a new future.

Is there an area in which God wants to renew and refresh you? Is there something you need to release so that God can accomplish some kingdom purposes in or through you? Some of us may need to let go of past accomplishments and victories and look for new opportunities to pursue, new dreams to be birthed, and new goals to strive after. You may be living under a cloud, thinking your best days have passed you by. It's not true! Don't give in to the lie that you've accomplished all that you can. There is purpose and significance in every day God grants you.

But the positive moments aren't the only ones that can trap us in the past. The bumps and bruises we acquire along life's journey can slow us down in the present as we carry the memories of a painful past. All too easily we can fixate on them and end up stuck, overcome with regret, or paralyzed with fear that an event could happen again.

These negative moments can take many shapes. It could be the moment you signed divorce papers. It could be the moment you heard harsh words of rejection from someone you love—a parent, a spouse, a child, a friend. It could be the moment you realized your business was failing. It could be the moment the phone rang with disturbing test results from your doctor's office.

Life can go from good to devastating in an instant. And we can't pretend that those moments don't have an impact on us. The danger is that if we choose to stay in those moments longer than we should, we'll miss out on today and jeopardize our future. But as much as a moment can affect our lives in a negative way, a single moment is often God's way of bringing a massive, power-packed opportunity our way that could change our lives in the best way possible. The question is, are we ready for it? Or are we tied up in the past?

Defining Moments

The roots of the word *moment* go back to Middle English through Anglo-French (*movere*, "to move") and ultimately to the Latin *momentum*, meaning "a particle sufficient to turn the scales." Movement and change are inherent in that original idea of a moment. When people refer to a moment, it's always about action, movement, and motion—not something fixed or stationary.

I love the word picture that comes to mind with this definition. Have you ever seen an old-fashioned scale that has a tray suspended on either side and is balanced at a central point? The scale of justice is often depicted this way. You can place a weight on one side and fill the other side with something until the two trays contain the same amount of weight. When the weights are equal, the trays balance perfectly and remain perfectly still. But if you start adding even the smallest bit more to one side, the scale starts teetering. If you keep adding weight to one side, there's that moment when the weight is enough to finally tip the scale. The tiniest particle, seemingly insignificant in and of itself, can make all the difference. It's the game changer that can tip the scale.

In our lives, that's what particular moments do: They change us. They can create motion where there was previously stillness. Moments can seem small, even insignificant or inconsequential, but they can hold explosive power—the power to tip the scale, to change a direction, to cause a course correction in our lives. From my experience, these defining moments are made up of three elements: opportunity, choice, and action. Let's consider the impact each one makes on determining what we get from the moments of our lives.

Opportunity

Opportunity can be defined as a favorable time or occasion, a situation that lends itself to advancement or success. God opens a door, brings a new relationship into your life, or gives you vision for something new that you didn't see before—a creative idea, a need in the marketplace, an awareness of future changes. Opportunities come in all shapes and sizes, and they don't always come when we plan on them or even when they're most convenient. In fact, sometimes on the surface they may even appear initially to be a problem. If we aren't careful, we can miss them altogether. The key is being prepared and being able to recognize an opportunity for what it is.

One of the reasons we miss out on opportunities is that we are looking back when we should be looking forward. So many good things await us—so much potential and so many possibilities—but if we're consumed by past failures or circumstances, we simply won't recognize the opportunities that may be right in front of us.

Choice

After we recognize an opportunity, we're positioned to unlock the potential within it. What will we choose to do with it? Will we have the faith and courage and strength to embrace it, to take hold of it and say yes to it? Will we take that next step?

Or will we let fear keep us stationary and frozen as that opportunity goes sailing by? Most opportunities have an expiration date. Will we be ready when a new opportunity arrives? Do we have the faith to open our hearts and minds and embrace the opportunity at hand? Will we make good decisions, or will we make careless choices based on temporary feelings and fleeting emotions?

God gave us incredible power when he gave us the ability to make choices on our own and choose the direction of our lives. This power of choice also makes us responsible for where our lives go. What we do with the defining moments we are given is up to us. And what we do with them determines the influence they will have on our lives for eternity.

Action

The third element found in a defining moment is action. Taking action is the biggest step and often the toughest. Many people get stuck in opportunity or paralyzed by choice when it comes to defining moments. We can see an opportunity and make the choice to embrace it, but if we never *do* anything, the other two steps really don't matter.

So many people cheat themselves out of a life-changing, defining moment because they don't act on the opportunity at hand. Sometimes they think the price is just too high. Opportunities don't cost anything. Embracing them doesn't cost anything either. But at the moment of action—that's when a price must be paid. Some people fear the cost of acting on an opportunity and never risk anything. Many people have great intentions, but it's those who act on them who will reap the benefits.

Living for the Moment

Renewal is an essential ingredient to momentum because our ways of doing things will never measure up to God's ways or produce the kind of progress in our lives that his ways will. The more we are transformed into his image, the more we are able to function in life as God intended—full of faith, winning life's challenges along the way, experiencing God's blessings, and being a blessing to others. Renewal brings momentum. *But* it requires that we leave behind the old and consistently embrace the new.

In Philippians 3:13–14, Paul provides this insight on what kept him moving forward: "No, dear brothers and sisters, I have not achieved it, but I focus on this one thing: Forgetting the past and looking forward to what lies ahead, I press on to reach the end of the race and receive the heavenly prize" (NLT). We have to be present and alert, forgetting the past and looking to the future, ready to take action in the divine moments God brings our way, or the transformation process will come to a halt and we will end up stuck.

Instead of *carpe diem*, "seize the day," maybe our motto should be *carpe momentum*, "seize the moment!" You see, there's a strong connection between "moment" and "momentum," not just in the definition and root of the word but in our lives. The moments in our lives are what produce momentum. When we string our moments together, our momentum builds. Momentum is motion caused by the moments in our lives. Momentum gains intensity as the defining moments of our lives accumulate. Every moment spent pushing forward builds on the moment before and carries the weight, the speed, the energy of it forward into the next. This crescendo of moments creates momentum.

The converse is true as well. Every moment spent in regret, worrying about the past, or reliving it can actually create reverse momentum and pull us away from hopeful futures. We cannot undo the past. God never intended for our lives to be defined by a single moment or season.

If you're feeling trapped by a negative event or season in your life, the good news is that you can change. You don't have to let that experience or moment hold you captive any longer. You can overcome that obstacle, whether it's a hurt, a failure, an unmet expectation, or a season of life that has left you tired and lacking motivation. But it requires a choice on your part. You can hold on to your past, forfeiting the renewal process God offers to produce progress and momentum in your life. Or you can surrender your past and allow God to bring the change and newness into your life you need to enter a new season and accomplish his plans for your life.

Let It Go

There are many stories in the Bible of people who overcame past failures and went on to do great things for God. The story of Joseph illustrates this perfectly. When Joseph was a young boy, his brothers were jealous of him because he was their father's favorite. When Joseph shared a dream that his brothers would bow down to him, they were overcome with anger, and when they had the chance, they threw him into a pit. Soon after, they sold him into slavery—into a life of terrible hardship and mistreatment. Can you imagine what it must have been like to be so hated by your family that they would sell you into slavery?

Joseph was sold to a wealthy Egyptian man named Potiphar, the captain of Pharaoh's guards, and found favor with him. Joseph was put in charge of everything in Potiphar's household. But then Potiphar's wife tried to seduce him. When he refused her advances and ran away, she accused Joseph of trying to rape her. Her accusation landed him in prison.

In prison, Joseph refused to become a victim of circumstance. His integrity impressed the warden, and he found favor with the guards. This favor allowed him the opportunity to interpret the dreams of two officers. Two years later, Pharaoh had a dream that no one could interpret. The cup bearer (one of the officers) remembered how Joseph had interpreted his dream in prison and told Pharaoh.

Joseph was brought before Pharaoh and told him what his dream meant. Their crops would be abundant for seven years, but then seven years of famine would follow. But not only that, Joseph also gave Pharaoh a master plan for saving the nation from the coming famine. Pharaoh was so impressed that he made Joseph second in command. Joseph, a foreigner and an imprisoned slave, was elevated to the second highest position of influence and power in the land.

Years later, Joseph's family in Israel was starving and went to Egypt for food. As second in command and in charge of all the food distribution during the seven-year famine, Joseph had the perfect opportunity to get revenge on his brothers for what they had done to him. He could have rejected them, humiliated them, even killed them, but instead he cared for them, forgave them, and provided for their needs.

Joseph's life was a series of ups and downs—seemingly tragic events that worked together to put him in a place of prominence and influence. His position of authority not only saved his family but also saved an entire nation.

If Joseph had allowed any of those individual moments of setback and tragedy to define his life, imagine how different his life would have been. A nation would have suffered famine and possibly been wiped out. At the minimum, his family might have perished, ending its legacy. But Joseph kept his heart faithful and trusted in God's provision. The result was that he was able to navigate each season successfully and keep making progress in life.

Just as he did in Joseph's life, God can take the difficult times in your life and use them to fulfill his purpose. But you must be willing to let go of the past. Whom do you need to forgive? What do you need to release? Where is God calling you to go? Allow God to renew you.

God is at work in your life right now, even as you are reading these words on the page. He is doing a new thing. You can't move forward if you're facing the past. It's time to turn and face the future. Keep your eyes on the prize, and you'll be amazed at where God leads you!

8

Time for a Change

Bad habits are like a comfortable bed, easy
to get into, but hard to get out of.

Anonymous

I love Starbucks. I still remember when I took my first sip—it
changed my life! I could drink Starbucks coffee all day long—
and sometimes I do. Not too long ago, I loaded my Starbucks
card with enough money to get me through the week. Two
days later when I got to the register to pay, the card was empty.
I had the clerk run it again just to double-check because I
was sure I couldn't have used it up that fast. Wrong. When
I thought back over the previous couple of days, I realized
that, sure enough, I'd hit Starbucks several more times than
I had originally thought.

I've learned that I have to watch myself. If I'm not careful, I can get caught up in a bad habit. Now there's nothing
wrong with a cup of coffee, but there is something wrong
when my desire for coffee becomes an obsession.

No matter what our habits may be, when we allow them to grow unchecked, they usually take up more and more room in our lives and take us farther away from God.

We usually grow into bad habits. No one wakes up one day and thinks, *I'm going to become a prescription drug addict today* or *I'm going to be the biggest gossip in the entire office.* No, habits develop over time. Is there an area of your life that's drifted out of control? Do you ever feel like you're being influenced by something you wish you could change?

Battle Plan

If we are going to be people who are living out what Jesus prayed in the Lord's Prayer—working to establish God's kingdom on earth and experiencing his power at work in our lives—we've got to allow God's renewing power to bring freedom into the areas that hold us back. Bad habits and negative patterns in our lives have a limiting effect.

Breaking free from old habits is similar to changing our thoughts because behavior is a product of our thinking. We change our thoughts internally and go the extra step to change our action externally. When we give God access to the core, inner parts of our lives, he begins to renew us deep within by confronting the habits and patterns in our lives that trip us up over and over again.

Often, we know we should change and even want to change, but we have trouble making any progress. In order to move forward in our lives, we must identify bad habits, or strongholds as the Bible often calls them, and take steps to confront them.

Stronghold is another word for *fortification*, which originally referred to the forts along Middle Eastern trade routes. Soldiers would use the forts to provide protection from caravans of thieves. The forts were places where the soldiers could "hold strong." It allowed the soldiers within to hold their current position unthreatened by opposing forces. Even with great force, it was difficult to get to them once they were in their stronghold. Strongholds in our lives create walls around our bad habits and poor mind-sets, fortifying them against our best efforts to destroy them. Once they are established, they are tough to break down and destroy.

The strongholds in our lives form around unbelief or wrong belief. Most negative habits and strongholds are built from bricks of fear on a foundation of faulty thinking. We'll never reach our destination unless we let God into those deep places and work alongside him to break down our strongholds. Let's look at some common strongholds that many of us deal with.

Not To Worry

One of the most prevalent strongholds is fear. It takes many forms—fear of failure, fear of rejection, fear of a thousand other things. Some bad habits are so common in our society that they may seem invisible to us. Worry is one of the most common, and it's based in fear. It robs so many people of the gifts God has for them.

People worry about the future. They worry about money. About finding a job. About keeping a job. About their health. About their safety. About their kids. About their relationships.

We can't enjoy what we have in the present if we're worried about losing it. We can't focus on the future if we're consumed with worry about today. "Anxiety weighs down the heart" (Prov. 12:25 TNIV). It's hard to make progress when we're carrying the heavy burden of worry all the time.

Sure, it's normal to be concerned about things we value— if we weren't concerned, it would mean we didn't care. It's normal to feel anxious before taking a test or making a big presentation. It's not a bad thing to get concerned when we start slipping on our budget. The healthy kind of anxiety moves us to responsible action—to get a job so we can pay our rent, to show up to our job so we don't get fired, to pay our bills so our electricity stays on. But we can so quickly slip from healthy anxiety into harmful worry.

Worry can become a stronghold in our lives, eating up large amounts of time and energy. Worry distorts our perspective and shrinks our world—we end up focusing on the minors and forgetting about the majors. Healthy anxiety compels and motivates us, while harmful worry drives and consumes and dominates us. When our worry is greater than our faith and we begin to live in fear, driven and dominated by the what-ifs and lacking a foundation of confidence in God, that's when we're in trouble.

Jesus knew it would be easy for us to get consumed with the things that fill our daily lives. He reminds us to keep it simple. "That is why I tell you not to worry about everyday life—whether you have enough food and drink, or enough clothes to wear. Isn't life more than food, and your body more than clothing? . . . So don't worry about tomorrow, for tomorrow will bring its own worries. Today's trouble is enough for today" (Matt. 6:25, 34 NLT).

Jesus asked, "Why do you have so little faith?" When we worry, we choose to look at the what-ifs more than God's Word and his promises to us. Worry distracts us and erodes our faith and keeps us from moving confidently in the direction of our dreams. If we don't learn to get a handle on it, worry will consume us, dominating our thoughts and controlling our actions.

In the last chapter, we talked about eliminating poor thinking. Choosing to focus our thoughts on the right things is a key to escaping the grip of worry. Another major strategy for deflating our anxiety is prayer. When we're in the habit of praying—communicating with God—we not only get to share with him our worries, concerns, and fears, but we also get to listen to what he's telling us and receive his comfort and guidance.

"Don't worry about anything; instead, pray about everything. Tell God what you need, and thank him for all he has done. Then you will experience God's peace, which exceeds anything we can understand. His peace will guard your hearts and minds as you live in Christ Jesus" (Phil. 4:6–7 NLT). This is a great pattern for dealing with worry in our lives. God can, and will, give us peace when we take our worries to him in prayer.

Mad about You

Anger plagues many people. In and of itself, anger is not a sin or a stronghold, but people who allow themselves to get angry often find that sin and strongholds aren't far behind. Scripture is clear that "in your anger do not sin" (Eph. 4:26). It is also clear that Jesus himself got angry several times and yet never sinned. For instance, Jesus felt angry when the moneychangers were disrespecting his Father's house with their greed, and so he drove them away.

This helps us make a distinction between anger that's justified and anger that's sinful. When we get angry about something that angers the heart of God and take positive action because of it, that is righteous anger. We're allowing God to direct our anger to make a change, correct a mistake, or right an injustice.

The truth is that some of us need to get a little angry. Is your marriage struggling? Get angry and do something about it. I'm not saying you should get mad at your spouse, but you should get angry with the enemy, who is working his plan to undermine something holy. Are you on autopilot in your parenting? Then get angry. It's time to stop being indifferent and parenting by default and start engaging your children's hearts and their need to know God.

Too many Christians have no passion or enthusiasm about the things of God and then wonder why they're stuck. Righteous anger can be a powerful catalyst in helping us experience renewal and get unstuck.

Sinful anger is selfish anger. It is anger driven by our own self-interests, often expressed in harmful, damaging ways. We either stew in our angry emotions—becoming bitter, vengeful, and resentful—or we spew out toxic emotions in the form of actions or words that scar those around us.

Such anger can also be physically harmful. Anger damages our bodies because it literally acts as poison within us. Just look at a few of the things that have been linked to unmanaged anger:[1]

- headache
- digestion problems
- abdominal pain
- insomnia
- increased anxiety
- depression
- high blood pressure
- eczema and other skin problems
- heart attack
- stroke

The *Harvard University Gazette* published an article with these amazing findings: "Researchers at Johns Hopkins School of Medicine tracked 1,055 medical students for 36 years. Compared with cooler heads, the hotheads were six times more likely to suffer heart attacks by age 55 and three times more likely to develop any form of heart or blood vessel disease."[2] The damage that comes from unchecked anger can be catastrophic to our health, our relationship with our spouses or kids, and even our careers. Scripture tells us that we shouldn't let the sun go down on our anger, that we should deal with disputes immediately rather than allowing them to build up inside.

Resentment is in the same family as anger—I like to think of it as a cousin. It's like the residue that anger leaves after the heat of the moment has passed. It can build up and be just as damaging. I've seen resentment cause damage in many marriages. It can bring people to a standstill and begin to destroy what once was a happy marriage.

The Bible tells us that when we remain angry or hold on to resentment we give the devil a foothold. The word *foothold* literally means a physical space, a room. Don't give the enemy a guest room in your heart. He can come in through the open door of your anger if you don't address the cause. Deal with the root of the issue. Talk it out if you need to. Ask God to help you deal with the issues in your heart that trigger your anger. As you do, you'll begin to close the door on sinful anger in your life.

Solving the Puzzle

God doesn't want us to be tied up by things like anger and worry—or by lust, addiction, or any other stronghold. His plan is for us to walk in freedom. In Scripture, we usually find two types of freedom, instant and progressive.

Instant freedom is the best kind; we're instantly set free. This is what happens to our spirits when we receive Christ. Sometimes it happens in other areas as well. Some people are miraculously delivered from a drug or alcohol addiction with no withdrawal. Some experience emotional freedom from scars they've carried for years and are restored instantly to wholeness by the power of God. The God we serve can do anything!

We can and should believe in instant freedom, but we also need to know that most times achieving and walking in freedom take effort and commitment on our part. This kind of freedom, progressive freedom, requires more from us. Much of the freedom that has come into my life has come this way. It's like pieces of a puzzle that start coming together. A piece fits here, and God brings the next piece, and we start working it out. If we think about it, this makes sense. If we spend our lives without Jesus, getting all tied up in knots, making a commitment to live for him doesn't necessarily mean that all the knots will miraculously come untied. We have to take steps of obedience and faith as the Holy Spirit leads us forward.

Maybe you've heard the story about the father who was trying to take a nap one Sunday afternoon. His young son kept coming to him with those famous words, "Daddy, I'm bored." So his father found a picture in the Sunday newspaper of a world map. Using a pair of scissors, he cut up the map into jagged pieces and handed them to the little boy.

"Okay, here's a puzzle. I want you to put all the pieces together to form a map of the world." Returning to his spot on the sofa, the dad thought he'd have at least an hour to nap before his son finished.

About ten minutes later, the boy woke him up, saying, "Daddy, I did it! I put all the pieces of the puzzle together." The man was skeptical, but sure enough, the world map was complete.

"Wow, son, how did you do that?" he asked.

The little boy replied, "Well, there was a picture of a person on the other side. When I got my person put back together, the world looked just fine!"

When you take obedient steps, one at a time, God helps you put the pieces of your life back together. With his help, it's amazing how much better your world begins to look. But it takes you working with God's help for the pieces to fit.

It's the age-old collaboration. God does his part, and we have to do our part. We need God's power, *and* we need our willpower. We can't do his part, and he's not going to do our part. Old habits die hard. Things don't always change overnight. We have to be willing to put in the work over time and commit to the process. Too often we want the promises of God, but we don't want to commit to the steps required to receive them.

We've got to put effort into learning God's Word, make the changes it tells us to, and stay faithful to the process. That's when freedom begins to come. "I will walk about in freedom, for I have sought out your precepts" (Ps. 119:45).

Freedom Fighters

Freedom doesn't come without a fight. It's a benefit that has been made available to us as children of God, but we have to be willing to press on to win the war against the negative habits and behaviors that hold us back from God's best. It's not always easy, but it's a fight worth fighting. Keep taking your next step . . . and then the next and the next. "So let's not get tired of doing what is good. At just the right time we will reap a harvest of blessing if we don't give up" (Gal. 6:9 NLT). Don't grow weary on your quest for renewal. The rewards will be well worth it.

One of the most powerful things we can do is make our own declaration of independence from the strongholds in our lives. We ask for God's power to come into our lives. We draw a line in the sand and decide we're not going back. We step out of the old and into the new. As we do, we position ourselves to move into a fresh new future that's full of hope and possibility.

One step forward: God, I know that my thoughts and ways of doing things are different from yours. Show me specific areas that you want to change and make new. I don't want to hold on to things that would keep me from moving forward. Give me the strength and self-discipline to handle myself—my thoughts, my actions, my attitude, my spirit, and my emotions—in a way that is pleasing to you. Make me new from the inside out. Thank you that your renewing power is at work in my life, helping me be all that you've called me to be.

RELEASE

BREAKING BARRIERS
TO RECEIVE GOD'S BLESSINGS

9

Our Daily Bread

Give us today our daily bread.
Matthew 6:11

A few years ago, my wife and I realized we were starting to outgrow our house. It was a great little house that we'd moved into not long after settling in Memphis to start a church. At the time, we were about to have our first child, and this house seemed perfect. We loved it, and Leslie did an amazing job decorating it and making it feel cozy and special. It was our nest, a shelter that always made us glad to come home. We thought we could live there forever.

Two kids and ten years later, however, we were feeling cramped. It's like when you wake up one morning, step on a Lego, stumble over a couple of backpacks, realize you can't find the book that you left with all the other books in a stack near your desk in a corner of the bedroom, and . . . you get the picture. Don't get me wrong—Leslie's a great housekeeper and did an amazing job keeping us clean, neat, and organized. It just seemed that four people (and a dog) had a lot more stuff than a young married couple who had just returned from the mission field in Africa. It was time to find a larger home. We put our house on the market and started looking at other places.

Like many people in recent years, we weren't looking at an ideal situation when it came to selling. The economic downturn that occurred in 2008 coincided with our desire to sell. Regardless, we decided to go for it.

Then it happened.

No, we didn't sell our house, but we found one we absolutely loved and wanted to buy. It was the perfect size and location and was a really good price. We weren't sure what to do.

We prayed about it and got some input from people in real estate. We ran the numbers and figured out that we could stretch things and manage to pay for both places for a few months until our old home sold. So we took a chance and moved forward with the purchase of the house we'd found.

It ended up taking much longer than a few months for our old place to sell—in fact, a year passed before we had a buyer. During that time, we waited and wondered when our house would sell. We made two house payments each month, which got a little frustrating at times. And there were some times when we second-guessed our decision.

I'm sure many of you can relate. Many people were unable or are still unable to sell homes that have been on the market for a long time. Other people have lost their homes to foreclosure or been forced to sell at a considerable loss. As difficult as it may seem sometimes, we have to stay committed to trusting God and doing things his way, even in the midst of challenging situations.

So far we've looked at the principles of honor and renewal that emerge from the Lord's Prayer. Now we're going to dive deep into a very practical portion of the Lord's Prayer. Jesus tells us to pray, "Give us today our daily bread." This is much more than just asking for food to sustain our bodies and get us through that day. Jesus is telling us that God is the only one who can truly sustain us and give us what we need to live. He's giving us a principle by which to live our lives. It's the principle of release—putting ourselves in a position of trusting and relying on God to be our provider, the ultimate source of provision for *all* our needs, body, soul, and spirit.

It's important that we recognize the significance of what Jesus offers us by telling us to pray this way. Remember, this is the model he gave us for how to connect and communicate with our Father every day. God cares about our provision, and he wants us to bring our needs and requests to him as a regular part of our daily lives.

"Give us today our daily bread" communicates both a request and a statement. As we make this request, we approach God with humility and an understanding that we need him in this fundamental area of our lives. But we're also making a statement. We're acknowledging that we can go to God in confidence because we know what he's promised us. Joining our request with the recognition of our dependence on God positions us to receive his provision.

Money Matters

Provision naturally centers around one of the most significant and potentially complicated areas of our lives—our finances. If there's ever been a time of fear in the area of our finances, it's now. Money issues surround us every day. Some involve big decisions, such as whether to purchase or sell a home. Others are small, such as whether to buy our daily coffee. Either way, we can't avoid money matters in our lives, and for many people, money can be a source of ongoing stress.

If you do a little online research, it doesn't take long to realize how much we stress over money. Nearly 70 percent of Americans worry about money "all the time"![1] Just think about that. If you look around your neighborhood, the people in seven homes out of ten are worrying about money—right now, today. Then multiply that by the population of our great nation, and it's pretty alarming.

Even before the economic downturn, bankruptcies and foreclosures reached record highs—higher than any time in our country's history, including during the Great Depression and both World Wars. Here in Memphis, we have earned the infamous label of being the bankruptcy capital of the United States. Shelby County, Tennessee, processes more bankruptcies per capita than any other county or parish in the US.

And yet, strangely enough, even as our financial troubles skyrocket, people remain reluctant to admit there's a problem. Money is still a taboo subject with most people. Do you remember talking to your parents about money or asking your dad how much money he made? Maybe you got an earful like I did! He said, "Well, son, that's really no one's business." And then he went on to tell me how it's impolite and poor etiquette to ask people how much money they make.

I found a statistic that reinforces this reluctance people have to discuss their finances. A staggering 8 out of 10 people would rather talk about their weight than how much credit card debt they are carrying.[2] Can you believe that? This statistic reflects what a widespread issue this is and how much personal shame most people attach to their finances. It's an emotionally charged issue that strikes deep chords in virtually everyone.

God's Economy

The Bible is full of promises about our finances. God doesn't want us to spend all our time stressing about money. He doesn't want us to become stuck in the quicksand of financial desperation where so many people find themselves today. Did you know that almost eight hundred verses in the Bible deal with money and money management? The Bible has more to say about money than about heaven and hell combined. Just think about how important prayer is to the life of the believer, and yet God talks about money five times more. Out of the thirty-eight parables Jesus told, sixteen of them focus on money and money management.

Why? Because God knows this is a critical area of our lives. "Where your treasure is, there your heart will be also," Jesus said (Luke 12:34). Our finances can be an area of strength and a tool to help move us into our future and be a blessing to others. Or our finances can be the most frustrating, debilitating area of our lives, leaving us feeling defeated, paralyzed, and focused on ourselves. God doesn't intend for us to be crippled by money.

While some people and churches have taken biblical principles to the extreme, the truth is the Bible holds the keys we need to successfully manage our money.

God gives us a clear path to financial freedom. We can be *productive* in our endeavors, accomplishing the things that need to be done. Our finances can actually work for us instead of pulling us down and dragging us under.

We can be *peaceful*, viewing our finances as a testimony of God's presence in our lives. Money doesn't have to give us ulcers or keep us up at night. It doesn't have to be a source of constant anxiety and tension. We can have stability and security instead of financial chaos, if we're willing to trust God and follow his directions.

We can be *prosperous* in our financial matters, experiencing momentum and growth instead of paralysis and stagnation. God wants us to be healthy and strong in every area of our lives, not struggling and weak. He never intended for money to have the power to suck the energy out of all the other areas of our lives.

We need to believe God's promises and release our frustrations about the present, our regrets about the past, and our dread of the future. We really can't afford not to trust God in this area of our lives. The price of distrust is too high. Statistically, 57 percent of American marriages end in divorce, citing "financial problems" as the primary reason for the demise of their marriage.[3] Too much is at stake in our lives for us to ignore what God's Word says about our finances.

Monkey Business

As we've noted with the principles of honor and renewal, momentum in our lives requires collaboration with God. God requires us to do our part if we are to see him move in our lives. The same is true with the principle of release.

Our action initiates a God reaction in our lives, which means we must be proactive and take some first steps. This goes against the grain of how many of us manage our finances. So often we react where money is concerned, always playing catch-up and trying to recover from the last blow. We need to have a plan and a vision for our finances and then take some steps that will help us achieve our vision.

What we release determines what we receive. We're told in Galatians 6:7, "Do not be deceived. . . . A man reaps what he sows." If we don't like what we are seeing in our finances, we need to take a look at what we are releasing and make some changes. Where we are today is largely a product of the seeds we sowed yesterday. We have to make sure we are sowing good seeds.

This principle of release often seems counterintuitive to our natural way of thinking. We want to hold on to what we have. But just as a farmer must sow seeds if he wants to gain the harvest, we must be willing to release the things God asks us to release so we can receive all that he wants to give us. This means we have to let go of our way of doing things and trust God's way. If we live with a closefisted approach to our finances and fail to release the right things, we will miss out on God's provision.

The following story shows what can happen if we hold on to something so tightly even though it is keeping us stuck in place and is potentially destructive.

> Native tribes used to catch monkeys by hollowing out a co-conut and filling it with rice or other delicacies, then leaving it tethered to a tree for a monkey to find. A monkey would reach in and grab the desired delicacy and be trapped because the hole had been deliberately made just big enough for a flexible hand to enter but not for a closed fist to leave. In short order, the monkey went from getting his dinner to being someone else's dinner.
>
> Clearly it was not the coconut that was trapping the monkey. Rather the true trap was in the monkey's own mind, the monkey's greed, the monkey's attachment to his physical possessions, the monkey's unwillingness to "let go."[4]

Like the monkey in the trap, we want to hold tightly to what we want, never realizing that it's controlling us—and ultimately causing destruction in our lives. We work so hard to keep, but in God's kingdom, the key to moving forward is to release.

But we must release the right things. In the next few chapters, we'll look at some specific things we need to release. As we do our part to release what God tells us to release, we can be confident that he will do his part, providing his provision and the power we need to move forward.

10

In God We Trust

Having thus chosen our course, without
guile and with pure purpose, let us renew
our trust in God, and go forward without
fear and with manly hearts.

Abraham Lincoln

Recently, I was spending the morning studying at home, getting ready for the weekend's message in peace and quiet—
something that's pretty rare around our house. I was sitting
by a window that looks out over our backyard so I could
enjoy watching the birds at the feeder that Leslie set up. What
she's figured out is that premium birdseed is the best way to
attract the most beautiful, unique birds.

On this particular morning, I was studying and praying
when I heard a thunk followed by a loud scraping noise. I
looked up but didn't see anything outside, so I went back to
my notes. Then again—thunk, thunk—followed by more
furious scraping. I tried to ignore the sounds, but I have a bit

of ADD in my personality and the slightest distraction can steal my focus in an instant. I put my Bible down and got up to see what was going on.

When I got to the window, I saw the fattest, nastiest, mangiest squirrel I'd ever seen jumping from the corner of our roof onto Leslie's birdfeeder! He was huge—as big as a house cat—and as ugly as could be. So I tapped on the window to try to scare him away. He just stared at me as if to say, "Who are you and what do you want?" and then went right back to stuffing his face. I knocked on the window again a little harder, but this time he barely even turned his head.

I was a little annoyed, but at the same time, it was kind of funny watching this ridiculously bold, scrappy-looking animal blatantly making himself at home, helping himself to our birdseed.

I tried to go back to studying, but the distraction was too much. When I have to stay put and focus for long periods of time, I usually end up looking for some kind of a diversion. And this was just the thing. I decided to show him that I could play this little game he'd started . . . and I'd win.

I ran to the closet and grabbed my son's BB gun.

Once outside, I yelled at the squirrel, and he quickly scampered down the birdfeeder and ran several feet away. Guess I showed him, right? Wrong. Just as I turned to go back in the house, I saw a blur in the corner of my eye. Sure enough, he'd climbed back on the roof and jumped back on the feeder. I couldn't believe the nerve of that fat, mangy squirrel!

Sensing my intensity, my furry enemy looked me in the eye and then . . . stood there and ate more birdseed. That was the last straw! I double-pumped my son's air rifle and took aim. He must have known I meant business because just as I pulled the trigger he dove for the fence and made a run for it, sprinting along the top of the fence with lightning speed. And that's when I heard it—the pa-ping of the BB hitting something. *My neighbor's big, huge, beautiful bay window.*

Lean on Me

Unfortunately, shooting at the squirrel didn't solve my problem; it actually created another one. The same thing happens when we try to rely on ourselves, our own ideas, our own strength, or our own solutions. When we set our sights without seeking God's direction, trusting in our own abilities and reasoning to work our way out of a problem, we often create a bigger problem. Instead, we need to place our trust in an immovable, unchanging God who remains the same yesterday, today, and forever.

So many people are facing challenges when it comes to their finances, but what most of us forget is that the answer is right in front of us. Our US currency bears the motto "In God We Trust," but so often we don't follow this wisdom as we handle the very currency it's printed on.

We're all trusting in something, especially when it comes to our money, but we must ask ourselves if it's the right thing. Are we putting our fiscal confidence in our 401k or in the stock market? Are we placing all our future hopes on our retirement account? Or are we placing our trust in God for our daily bread, for our ongoing provision and ultimate necessities?

Trust is like an arrow. It needs to be aimed in the right direction before it's released. When we trust, in terms of our finances, we must aim at something that's solid and fixed, not the moving target of the Dow Jones or the roulette wheel. Our trust needs to be in a God who isn't surprised by an economic downturn, a God who isn't dependent on Wall Street and the latest unemployment data. If we're going to hit the mark and truly trust God, we must pay attention to how we take aim.

The Bible says, "Trust in the LORD with all your heart, and lean not on your own understanding; in all your ways acknowledge Him, and He shall direct your paths" (Prov. 3:5–6 NKJV). When we trust in something, we lean on it. For example, when we're tired and we believe a wall will hold us up, we lean on it, we rely on it. There is literally a shift that takes place. We shift our weight. We are no longer bearing it. We are allowing the wall to carry or bear the majority of it. We go from holding ourselves up to relying on the wall to hold us up. If that wall moves, we're in trouble! But if the wall does move and we don't fall, then we weren't really counting on it, we weren't really trusting in it to hold us up in the first place.

It's the same with our finances. We have to lean on God to the point where we are in a position of reliance upon him. Anything else means we're leaning on our own understanding, wisdom, and logic. And that's exactly what the Bible tells us *not* to do. We're placing our trust in our banker, our stockbroker, our wealth management advisor, our spouse, our boss, or our parents instead of God.

The Bible says we are to acknowledge him in *all* our ways. The word *acknowledge* means to recognize the importance or truth of something. When we recognize and accept the importance and truth of God in *all* our ways, that's when he makes our paths straight. He starts to lead us and guide us and keep us on track.

Notice a pattern? God is about us being "all in." I'm always amazed at those celebrity poker players on TV in the big tournaments. When they decide to go all in, they have to have tremendous confidence—either in the cards in their hand or in their ability to bluff. When we trust in God and go all in, we're not taking a gamble. He's a sure thing. We can fully trust in him.

When we release our trust, God releases his strength back to us. He tells us, "In quietness and trust is your strength" (Isa. 30:15). He's not talking about strength of personality or willpower. He's talking about an inner strength, an emotional strength, a spiritual strength fueled deep down inside by his Spirit within us.

Rise and Shine

Psalm 20 contains this great reminder: "Some trust in chariots and some in horses, but we trust in the name of the Lord our God" (v. 7). The psalmist is making a distinction. He's saying, as followers of God, there should be a difference in our lives. Other people might place their trust in their bank balance or stock portfolio, in real estate or other investments. But if we know Jesus and have a relationship with him, we must rely on the Lord our God as the foundation on which we build our lives, our relationships, and our resources. Others might trust in themselves and whatever else appears logical or feels safe. We need to trust in God regardless of whether it seems logical or feels comfortable.

Why? Because ultimately, everything else won't last and can't support us. God's Word and his principles are the only things that will consistently prove true in our lives. The psalmist explains: "They [those who trust in chariots and horses] are brought to their knees and fall, but we [those who trust in the name of the Lord our God] rise up and stand firm" (v. 8).

There may be seasons when we are tested by our circumstances. When the housing market collapses, do we panic? Do we fall into despair when we see how much we've lost in equity? Or is our hope in the Lord? Are we able to keep our chin up, press through with confidence, and manage our emotions when we take financial hits, even though it hurts and we may not know how things are going to work out? If we have an inner foundation of trust, we can absorb the shock that comes with an unstable, always changing economic environment. When we rely on God alone, things won't shake us to the point where we fall apart. This doesn't mean we're completely immune to circumstances, but we have the awesome peace that comes with knowing that they're within God's control. Circumstances may trip us up and try to push us around, but we will meet those circumstances with an immovable trust in an immovable God. We will rise up.

You may be facing difficult circumstances and challenges. Maybe you've asked for provision and you're doing the best you know how, but you're just not sure what to do or where to turn. It's in these times that you can release your trust and choose to have a "rise up" moment as God enables you to stand firm, just as the psalmist describes.

We will have setbacks. We will face challenges and circumstances. But we have hope because our trust is anchored in the Lord. Instead of *being* overcome, we can overcome.

How I See It

We have to really get this issue of trust settled in our hearts and minds if we want to have peace when it comes to our finances. Our hearts are settled when they are fixed on God, even if things aren't perfect. If we aren't willing to place our trust in God, we will limit our potential to move forward and become locked in to our current situation. In fact, one of the greatest causes of worry, especially in our finances, is misplaced trust.

Over my lifetime, I've met some very wealthy individuals. A good number of them still don't feel like they have enough money to do all that they want to do in life. It's not really about how much money we have or don't have. It's an issue of how we see money—our attitude and perspective toward it. Billy Graham said, "If a person gets his attitude toward money straight, it will help straighten out almost every other area in his life."[1]

One of the biggest shifts most people need to make in their mind-set or attitude toward money is learning how to trust God enough to follow his principles for handling money. We have to begin to build a new knowledge base that is rooted in what God has to say about money, not what the world around us says.

Jesus included this request for provision in his model prayer because he knew money would be an issue we would deal with constantly. Prayer helps us realign our priorities and change our perspectives so we can begin to see money the way God wants us to see it. If you're having trouble trusting God, prayer is a great place to start. Make it a habit to go to God in prayer for the things you need with the expectation that he is willing and able to meet your needs in every area of your life. God gives us fresh bread, fresh provision, not only in our finances but also in our spirits and souls, every day if we'll let him.

11

Trust and Obey

No principle is more noble, as there is none
more holy, than that of a true obedience.

Henry Giles

When I turned sixteen, I experienced every teenage driver's
dream. My dad and I went in together and bought a used
Ford Mustang. I had never really thought of myself as a car
guy, but it was love at first sight with this baby. It was white
with a red interior, and the way the headlights and grill were
positioned made it look like it had a tough face, like a snarling
beast. It was a Mustang 2 with a V8, and I barely had to tap
the accelerator to be instantly thrown back in my bucket seat
from the force. My buddies thought I had won the lottery
and rode with me every chance they got.

About two weeks after I had my Mustang, my friend and
I put together our party plans for the weekend. Like many
people at that age, we weren't making the best choices in
life and decided to break into his dad's office, steal a couple

bottles of whiskey that were gifts for clients, and get plastered. Could it get any better for two young guys than some Seagram's Seven and a sweet V8 ride? Well, we were about to find out.

I was driving on a service road heading into town when it started pouring down rain. We hadn't had anything to drink yet, but we were definitely distracted as we laughed and talked. As we approached another road, I barely noticed a yield sign.

Bam! I slammed into another car as I merged into his lane at fifty miles an hour. Ironically enough, the other car was a fully restored 1965 Mustang. After the crash it looked awful. It reminded me of an empty Coke can that somebody had tried to crush before tossing it into the trash. Its driver opened his door, and all I could see was the blood streaming from the guy's head. My friend and I had taken quite a jolt but miraculously seemed to have only a few cuts and bruises.

Soon the police and an ambulance were on the way, and I was in shock. My beautiful, new, supercharged Mustang with the amazing V8 looked even worse than the car I'd hit. In a matter of moments, my dream car became every teenage driver's nightmare. I was lucky to be alive . . . a fact my parents didn't let me forget as I faced the consequences of my poor choices for a long, long time.

Trust and Obey

As I grew older, I came to appreciate the fact that a yield sign is there for good reason. To avoid a collision like I experienced, drivers have to slow down, pay attention to what's happening, and yield their movement to the flow of traffic already in motion around them.

We have to do the same thing when it comes to the practices and principles God has put in place for us. We have to adjust our movement, yield to him, and obey the signs and instructions he gives. In the last chapter, we talked about the first thing we need to release—trust. The second thing we need to release is the power of obedience in our lives. When we release our obedience to God, he releases his abundance to us.

As a dad, I know how much I love to give my kids good gifts. It makes me happy. As our spiritual father, God is much more gracious and generous than we are. Just like I love to give my kids good things, he loves to give us good things. However, we have to do our part. We release obedience, and he releases abundance. We can't do his part, and he won't do our part.

God's blessing and favor don't just appear because we ask for them. We have to do more than offer up a prayer. When we truly put our faith in God and strive to know him, we're willing to walk in obedience to his instructions. We believe God and obey his Word, even when it isn't easy. The result is that the favor of God flows into our lives.

The Flavor of Favor

A timeless principle emerges from a story in the Bible about two brothers who each presented an offering to God. They both had something to give him. However, only one found favor with God.

"Now Abel kept flocks, and Cain worked the soil. In the course of time Cain brought some of the fruits of the soil as an offering to the LORD. But Abel brought fat portions from some of the firstborn of his flock. The LORD looked with favor on Abel and his offering, but on Cain and his offering he did not look with favor" (Gen. 4:2–5).

What we find in these verses is that what we offer God affects the favor that flows back to us. God looked with favor on Abel and his offering. He did not look with favor on Cain and his offering. Obviously, there was a crucial difference between the two offerings, but what was it?

The key is found in one little word right in the middle of verse 4: "firstborn." We're told, "Abel brought fat portions from some of the firstborn." Abel brought the *first* part. Cain brought *some*. The firstborn was considered the best. Abel may not have known if there would be a second- or third-born, but he gave the firstborn anyway. He wanted God to have his best. Right here we see the powerful principle of offering the first of everything. When we give God our best and bring him the first of everything, our action releases his favor.

Today we don't bring animals and vegetables to show our devotion to God, but the Bible does contain a principle that still applies to us. Leviticus 27:30 tells us, "A tithe of everything from the land, whether grain from the soil or fruit from the trees, belongs to the LORD." *Tithing* is a word you may have heard, but maybe you aren't familiar with what it means. Merriam-Webster's dictionary defines the word *tithe* as "a tenth part of something." Tithing is simply giving the first 10 percent of our income to God through the local church. Malachi 3:10 says it this way in the Amplified version: "Bring all the tithes (the whole tenth of your income) into the storehouse that there may be food in my house." God still intends for Christians to live by this principle, and it is fundamental to what we're talking about here. I believe it is the key to walking in favor and seeing God's grace flow into your finances.

The story about Cain and Abel illustrates the importance of giving the first of everything. God wants us to bring the first part to him because it belongs to him. He doesn't want just "some"—whatever we can spare or whatever's left over at the end of the month. If we want to honor God with our lives and if we say that he has first place in our lives, then shouldn't he have the best? But all too often, all that's left for him are the crumbs.

Leftovers

Leslie is an incredible cook and terrific hostess. She comes from a long line of cooks in her Italian family and has always loved to entertain and have people over. She'll usually start the preparations a day or two before the actual dinner, and she'll be in the kitchen all day, just before our guests arrive. She absolutely loves doing it and always cooks something amazing.

For our guests, my wife serves the very best she can make from the very best ingredients. And you know what? If there are any leftovers the next day, that's what the family gets served.

Can you imagine if it were the other way around? What if you invited friends over for dinner, and when they arrived, you told them to help themselves to anything in Tupperware while your family ate a fresh, warm, home-cooked meal? That's not how any of us would treat our guests. They're special, and we want to honor them and celebrate our time together by giving them the very best.

Unfortunately, not all of us have the same commitment when it comes to God. We spend what we want, how we want, then pay our bills and taxes, maybe save a little, and if there's any left, we give it to God. Instead of giving God our best, we give him our leftovers. That's not the way it works if we want to find favor with him and have his hand of blessing on our lives. He wants to be first in our lives and wants us to show our commitment by putting our money where our faith is.

Automatic Deposit

When you become a Christian, the first 10 percent of your income becomes a tool in your hand to release the favor of God to flow into your life. Now it would be one thing if God did an automatic withdrawal and took what was his, that first

111

10 percent, without asking and you didn't have any choice about it. In a lot of ways, that would be easier!

But God keeps it in your hands and leaves the choice about tithing up to you because he wants you to give it back with a willing spirit and to trust him with your life. "The purpose of tithing is to teach you always to put God first in your lives" (Deut. 14:23 TLB). Keeping God first requires faith—a lot of it sometimes. Everything in the kingdom of God operates according to faith. I've heard it said this way: "Faith is the currency of heaven." Faith is what moves God to act on our behalf.

Tithing is a good indication of the level of faith in our lives. God wants us to believe that living on 90 percent while acknowledging him as our source is a richer life than living on 100 percent. Tithing is an active step of faith that demonstrates whether or not we mean what we say. When we obey him, he makes an automatic deposit in us.

Releasing our obedience by tithing our first 10 percent positions us to receive God's abundance in our lives. But when we disobey by withholding our tithe, when we give God our leftovers—or worse, nothing at all—then we experience the consequences. In fact, God's Word goes so far as to call it a curse (Mal. 3:9).

Now that's a loaded word for many of us and may conjure up images of voodoo dolls and Harry Potter spells. But if you think about it, when we're stuck in place with our finances, doesn't it kind of feel as though we're cursed?

It's like being on a treadmill—you're constantly running, sweating, red-faced, and worn-out but never getting anywhere, no matter what you do. Financially, the same thing can happen. You're working hard, but you're still in the same place you were two years ago. Or worse, you're in more credit card debt, paying higher interest rates, and more stressed out than ever trying to pay your bills and keep your head above water. If that's not cursed, I don't know what is!

Reward Offered

If we want forward momentum in our finances, then we need God's favor. And if we want his favor, then we must demonstrate our faith in him by giving him what he tells us to give him. But this is about more than just our money. If we experience God's favor with our money, then we will experience it in other areas as well. Not only will God bless our finances, but he will also start moving in a powerful way in our lives.

I have seen it over and over again. As soon as we trust him enough to obey him, then things begin to change. We may not see the changes right away, and they may not always be in the form of financial gain. It won't be like a winning lottery ticket just fell from the sky or we inherited a million dollars. It will be better because it's the favor of God at work in our lives, giving us momentum we couldn't create on our own.

It's important to understand that blessings that flow back to us aren't all about money. In Matthew 4:4, Jesus tells us, "Man does not live on bread alone, but on every word that comes from the mouth of God." There is so much more to life than just the provision for our physical needs. There are blessings of protection, opportunity, health, new relationships, and more. God says, "'Bring the whole tithe into the storehouse, that there may be food in my house. Test me in this,' says the LORD Almighty, 'and see if I will not throw open the floodgates of heaven and pour out so much blessing that you will not have room enough for it'" (Mal. 3:10).

If you're serious about obeying God and allowing him to open the floodgates of heaven over your life, then I encourage you to follow God's instructions and make tithing a part of your life. There's no other financial strategy that can compare. If you don't have a local church where you attend regularly, one of the best things you can do is find a life-giving church, get planted, and start to tithe consistently.

The commitment to tithe really begins in your heart and mind. Take a moment to make a fresh commitment to keep

God first and honor him with every area of your life, including your finances. As you do, you are building a strong foundation of obedience that positions you to receive his abundance. Don't settle for giving God leftovers. Favor comes when we bring him our best.

12

Enough Is Enough

> Contentment makes poor men rich and dis-
> contentment makes rich men poor.
>
> Benjamin Franklin

After I recovered from the shock of totaling my new Mustang, the real tragedy revealed itself. Since I'd wrecked my
car, I had to share my dad's—a 1980 Ford Fairmont. It was
two-tone, white with a tan soft top. The sound system con-
sisted of an 8-track tape player that played only one tape. My
parents loved Freddy Fender, and the 8-track of his greatest
hits had gotten stuck in the player. Talk about "wasted days
and wasted nights"!

At the time, that was pretty much the lowest point in my
existence. To go from an incredible V8 Mustang to a Fairmont with a four-cylinder engine that whined if I went more
than sixty gave me emotional whiplash. I ended up having to
drive that car all through high school until I finally inherited

my sister's Escort, which is a story in itself. Compared to the Mustang, the family friendly Fairmont had no cool factor.

But of all the cars I had, the Fairmont is the one about which I have the most memories. When I was seventeen or eighteen, I was in a band with several of my buddies. We had played in New Orleans one night and were driving home to Baton Rouge with the music blasting. We started smelling smoke, but all the gauges looked fine, so we kept driving. What none of us realized was that the muffler was dragging the whole way home.

I'd hoped my dad would consider this the last straw for the Fairmont, but he just wired the muffler back on with a clothes hanger. Let me tell you, it was not the kind of ride that a teenage boy dreams of having, especially after he knows what it feels like to be behind the wheel of a Mustang. But the Fairmont got me where I needed to go. In fact, Leslie and I went on our first date in that old car. At least I knew she wasn't dating me for my car!

Sprinkler System

When it came down to it, I had a choice about my attitude toward driving my dad's Fairmont. I could grumble and complain, constantly wishing for my beloved Mustang and thinking about what might have been if I hadn't wrecked it. Or I could take responsibility for my poor decisions and now accept the reality before me.

I learned from driving a car I didn't like that I had a choice about my own contentment. I had a decision to make. I could focus on how bad I had it or be thankful I had a vehicle to drive, a fact that one of my car-less buddies constantly reminded me of. It's a choice you and I have each day as well.

One of the most important things we need to do when we ask God to "give us today our daily bread" is to release contentment into our lives. We have to make a conscious choice to cultivate gratitude and make it a predominant attitude in our lives. The people of Israel experienced God's provision for them when they wandered in the desert for forty years. Each day, he gave them manna, which scholars tell us was a bread-like substance. It couldn't be preserved or stored; it was just enough for that day. And then the next morning, more would appear, just enough for that day. They had to be content with the fact that God's provision for them came day by day. In many areas of our lives, this is how God's provision comes too—not all at once but a little bit each day, right as we need it.

God knows how quickly we lose sight of what we have and start focusing on what we don't have. It's always easier to look over the fence and think our neighbor's grass is greener than to water our own lawn. When we start to despise what we have or get caught up in our desire for what we don't have, we take what we *do* have for granted. The truth is that if we would stop looking at what someone else has and value what we have and do the best we can with it, it would probably start to look better. Then we would enjoy it a whole lot more. Releasing contentment is like a sprinkler system for our own yard that keeps our grass just as green as that on the other side of the fence.

It's easy for us to fall into the mind-set that tells us we always "need" more. We tell ourselves that once we're financially secure we'll feel at peace and be happy. We think that the more we have the more secure and satisfied we'll be. Ultimately, this is not true. And even if we can provide food, shelter, and comfort for ourselves, we can never find true satisfaction in anything other than God.

The "daily bread" we request from God shouldn't just be about our physical and material needs. Our lives aren't measured by our possessions—there's so much more to life than material things. One of the most significant things that God's provision includes is his presence in our lives. We can't truly experience a full and satisfying life without it. It's what feeds our spirits and sustains our souls. When we go to God as the source for our spiritual and emotional needs, doing so enables us to experience a contentment that transcends what we eat or wear or where we live. There's a satisfaction that our souls and spirits long for that can be found only in him.

Rest Period

When we do our part to release contentment, God releases rest back to us. When we experience rest in our spirits, we feel refreshed and renewed, filled with new energy and a passion for life. And having rest in our lives doesn't mean being lazy or inactive. That's physical rest—like taking a nap or chilling out on the couch while watching a movie. The kind of rest God releases is spiritual rest, rest for our souls. "So there is a special rest still waiting for the people of God. For all who have entered into God's rest have rested from their labors, just as God did after creating the world. So let us do our best to enter that rest" (Heb. 4:9–11 NLT).

When we release contentment in our lives, through a conscious choice and commitment, then we can receive that special rest of God deep down in our spirits. We experience freedom from striving and working to gain his or anyone else's approval. We're no longer driven by what other people think.

When we don't choose contentment and instead chase after all that we don't have, we end up restless, tired, anxious, and exhausted. We feel frustrated and tense. We worry about the future and often lose what we already have. We begin looking for something, or someone, that we think can satisfy us.

This is why so many people are always in what I call "shopping mode." They've had their car only a year, but they're ready to trade it in. They just moved into a new house a couple of years ago but want to upgrade. They're always looking for a better job. They tire of friends—and unfortunately, sometimes spouses—quickly. When the "new" wears off, they move on, again and again and again.

This kind of restlessness will eat away at our peace and rob us of our joy. Nothing is ever enough. We'll be constantly scanning, comparing, researching, and looking ahead at the next big thing and how we can get it. With this kind of approach, there's never time to stop and enjoy this moment right here, right now, today. It's only when we understand the power of releasing contentment that we can tap into the spiritual rest and peace that will allow us to enjoy today while we look forward to tomorrow.

Contentment Killers

If we truly want to be content, we're going to have to deal with the contentment killers in our lives. One of the biggest contentment killers is comparison. We look at what someone else has and begin to feel ungrateful for what we have. Soon we've convinced ourselves that we "need" what everyone else seems to have. The truth, of course, is that we have very few actual needs. We throw that word *need* around a lot, but most of the time we're actually saying we *want* something.

Have you ever really listened to the things we say we need? "I really *need* a new iPhone." "I really *need* some new clothes—I don't have anything to wear!" "I really *need* a new car" (especially after putting up with that Ford Fairmont for so long!). But this is what I've found. Even if we get what we think we need, it's not enough, and we're on to the next thing on our list. We have a little saying at our house: "No comparing. No complaining." It's easier said than done, and I don't always do it perfectly, but it helps me not get carried away in comparison.

Impatience is another contentment killer. Our culture demands instant gratification. If we have to wait thirty seconds for a video to load on the internet, we're frustrated at how slow it is. We want what others have and we want it now. Often, comparison and impatience work together and produce envy in us. Envy will rob us of the blessings we have right now. We have to remember that God knows what we need and what's best for us and that his timing is perfect.

It's okay to want to move beyond where we are now, but we must be careful that we don't get so far ahead of ourselves (and God) that we're frustrated and disgruntled with where we are and what we have today. Quite possibly, some of what we have now was what we longed for and wanted so badly last year. Instead of growing more content and satisfied with where we are, we only grow more restless and frustrated over where we want to be.

Jailhouse Rock

I'm convinced that contentment may be one of the most powerful attitudes we can cultivate in our lives. One particular man in Scripture, Paul, had a strong understanding of what it means to be content. Writing from a jail cell to friends at the church in Philippi, he was surprisingly calm and full of contentment:

> I was made very happy in the Lord that now you have revived your interest in my welfare after so long a time; you were indeed thinking of me, but you had no opportunity to show it.
>
> Not that I am implying that I was in any personal want, for I have learned how to be content (satisfied to the point where I am not disturbed or disquieted) in whatever state I am.
>
> I know how to be abased and live humbly in straitened circumstances, and I know also how to enjoy plenty and live in abundance. I have learned in any and all circumstances the secret of facing every situation, whether well-fed or going hungry, having a sufficiency and enough to spare or going without and being in want.
>
> I have strength for all things in Christ Who empowers me [I am ready for anything and equal to anything through Him

Who infuses inner strength into me; I am self-sufficient in Christ's sufficiency]. (Phil. 4:10–13 AMP)

Since he wrote this from prison, it's safe to say that Paul had earned the right to talk about this subject. Even as he wrote these very words in extremely difficult circumstances, he was putting contentment into practice. His definition of contentment meant "satisfied to the point where I am not disturbed or disquieted." You could also define contentment this way: "an attitude of satisfaction that arises from an inward disposition of freedom." Paul had the kind of freedom no jail cell could contain. He was free from the hold of greed, comparison, entitlement, and frustration because his desire for Jesus exceeded his desire for material comforts and ideal circumstances.

So few of us know how to live in a state of true contentment like Paul describes here. Most of us battle with a sense of dissatisfaction with some aspect of our lives, whether it's how we look, where we live, our achievements, our relationships, or our opportunities. And unfortunately, this lack of contentment robs us of being able to enjoy all that we have in the present—where we are, the people God has given us, and how he provides each day. Discontentment keeps us stuck.

"Godliness with contentment is great gain" (1 Tim. 6:6). Some people mistake contentment for indifference, thinking that they don't really need to aspire to change their circumstances or work to move forward in life. But when we're pursuing godliness, a commitment to the things that matter to God, we're filled with passion and a desire to do great things for God. In writing to the Philippians, Paul himself indicates that while he's content in all things, he's also moving forward in life, running the good race and pressing on to achieve the goals God has set before him. As Joyce Meyer puts it, you have to enjoy where you are on the way to where you're going.[1]

The Art of Contentment

Paul's example in Philippians provides three important applications. First, contentment is learned. He said, "I have *learned* to be content" (4:11). It's not a one-time, feel-good experience. It's not dependent on the kind of personality we have. It's not a divine gift that God bestows only on some people. It's not a fruit of the Spirit, and it doesn't just happen naturally. Contentment is a commitment. It's a choice we make every day. We have to put forth some effort in order to learn how to guard our hearts and manage our mind, will, and emotions so they stay healthy.

Second, Paul indicated that contentment provided him with the know-how to deal with life's ups and downs. Because he had learned the art of contentment, Paul wasn't afraid of being in jail or worried about whether or when he would be released. It's why he could write with the kind of confidence and assurance that we see in his letter. He was able to navigate the hard situations that arose in his life with clarity and composure. He didn't fall apart.

Finally, contentment comes from within. It shouldn't be dependent on our external circumstances and the situations we're facing at the moment. Paul said he had strength in Christ for all things, right then and there. He had enough because Christ is enough. The rest is secondary. His level of satisfaction wasn't based on how well things went or how comfortable he was. He wasn't concerned with how much money he had or whether he would survive another beating or shipwreck. He had confidence, inner fortitude, and stamina that flowed out of his love for God and his commitment to follow Jesus.

We can enjoy the same kind of contentment Paul experienced if we're willing to choose it, practice it, and live it out every day. When we learn to be grateful and satisfied with the daily bread God provides, our attitude releases God's rest in our souls. As we maintain the balance between contentment and godly passion for growth and expansion, we'll see the "great gain" that Paul talks about. As a result, we will naturally find ourselves moving forward, driven by something much more powerful than what we are working to achieve. When we practice contentment, we're running on strength we can find only in God.

One step forward: Heavenly Father, thank you for all the blessings you've given me. Help me to recognize them and be thankful for what you've given me today. I want to have your perspective in the area of my finances. I will not worry but instead place my faith in you to meet my every need, physically, spiritually, and emotionally. I choose to remember your promises and release trust, obedience, and contentment. I know that as I do you will release your strength, abundance, and rest back into my life.

FORGIVENESS

LIVING BY GOD'S GRACE
AND EXTENDING IT TO OTHERS

13

Forgive Our Debts

Forgive us our debts, as we also have forgiven
our debtors.

Matthew 6:12

For most of the forty-plus years my parents were married,
they met for coffee almost every weekday. Even though they
had two cars (well, unless I was borrowing the Fairmont),
they usually drove everywhere together—long before going
green and saving on gas made it popular. Most days my mom
and dad would leave early enough to have coffee together
at Highlands Coffee Shop on Chimes Street near the LSU
campus. After they finished, my dad would walk to campus
and Mom would drive to work.

After work, Dad would walk back to the coffee shop to
meet Mom, they would talk about the day over another cup
of coffee, and then they would head home together. My parents didn't have to arrange their day this way, but they did for

as long as I can remember. Anyone who saw them together instantly recognized the bond, the love, and the connection.

So much so that when students working there saw my dad sitting with this attractive woman, smiling, laughing, and talking . . . well, they just assumed he was having an affair. He never wore his wedding ring, and really, who meets for coffee twice a day with their spouse? The students working at the coffee shop eventually confessed to my parents that they had assumed my dad and his "friend" were both married, but it never crossed their minds that they were married to each other!

A Lesson in Love

It's pretty incredible when you think about it. For more than forty years of marriage, my parents just loved being together. And they couldn't have been more different, even in appearance. Dad looked the part of a mad scientist with his crazy hair, his pipe, and the front pockets of his shirts always ink stained where his pens had leaked. He was strong willed, opinionated, always had dirty hands from working on things—and did I mention strong willed? He was an incredible man for whom I have so much love and respect in my heart, but, oh, the stories my family could tell!

If my father was outspoken and always in charge, then my mom was his perfect complement—meek and mild, soft and compassionate. She was a CPA, very detail oriented and meticulous about her appearance. Unlike my dad, she always looked well put together with her perfectly pressed clothing. Their relationship wasn't perfect, but they loved each other and were committed to each other until my dad passed away. One of the keys to their love and longevity could probably be summed up in a single word: forgiveness.

I can imagine that in forty-plus years of marriage there are going to be some situations that require forgiveness. After four years—let alone *forty*—many people aren't even together anymore. Or if they are, many are just going through the motions, harboring hidden resentments and secret grudges, living as roommates and not husband and wife. No matter what kind of relationship, over time there will inevitably be mistakes made and feelings hurt.

If we want to navigate our relationships and our lives well, we're going to need to be good forgivers and good forgetters. If we aren't willing to forgive, then we will find ourselves encountering one of the biggest obstacles to the abundant, joyful life Jesus promised us.

Forgiveness was an ingredient of a successful marriage for my parents and one of the keys that allowed them to keep moving forward in their relationship. If at one point either of them had failed to forgive, the relationship would have begun to lose momentum.

All of us, in one capacity or another, are confronted with the issue of forgiveness on an almost daily basis. Whether it's something large like the betrayal of a spouse or something smaller like a rude comment from the guy in the cubicle next to us at work, we all encounter pain and disappointment at the hands of others.

We need to *receive* forgiveness, and we need to *release* forgiveness. We're told to ask God to forgive us our debts, or our sins, and in the same breath instructed to make sure we've forgiven our debtors, or those who have sinned against us in our lives. Forgiveness is twofold. It's vertical, between us and God, and it's horizontal, between us and others. We need both in order to keep our relationship with our Father unhindered.

Ask and You Shall Receive

Let's consider God's forgiveness toward us. Jesus tells us to ask our Father to "forgive us our debts." We must first come to God for forgiveness. We've all sinned. None of us is perfect, and we've all "fallen short of God's standard" (Rom. 3:23 NLT).

The unbelievably good news is that God can and will forgive us and make us clean. Our Father's mercy, grace, and love toward us are so great that he continues to forgive us, cleanse us, and heal us, even when we mess up again and again. God knows the things going on in our lives that we're not proud of, the secret habits we're ashamed of, the selfish choices we make that don't honor him. But his mercy is never failing and his love has no end. No matter what we've done and no matter what we're doing, God can forgive us! With our forgiveness in Christ, there's an amazing release that takes place within us. Nothing, absolutely nothing is beyond his power and ability to forgive—even the sins that we might label unforgivable by human standards such as murder, rape, abuse, or adultery. He's able to cleanse us of any and every sin and wrongdoing. Nothing is too big.

Once God has forgiven us, our sins are totally removed. The Bible says, "He has removed our sins as far from us as the east is from the west" (Ps. 103:12 NLT). We experience a release of the burden that sin brings into our lives. When we're forgiven, the weight of sin is gone. We're no longer tied down. "If we confess our sins, he is faithful and just and will forgive us our sins and purify us from all unrighteousness" (1 John 1:9). God will forgive us, cleanse us, and set us free.

God is filled with love for us, and he's ready to forgive us—all we have to do is ask. Sometimes we don't come to God because we know what we're doing is wrong and we are filled with shame. But we can't ever let shame stand in the way of coming to God. If we have something in our lives that needs forgiveness, the worst thing we can do is run from God or remain tangled up in that sin.

Instead of running *from* him, we need to run *to* him and know he will always receive us. Even if he doesn't love what we're doing, he always loves us and his arms are open wide.

"O Lord, you are so good, so ready to forgive, so full of unfailing love for all who ask for your help" (Ps. 86:5 NLT).

If we're wrestling with guilt and shame and don't want to face him to ask for forgiveness, there are three things we should remember. First, he forgives us instantly. When we ask him to forgive us, he doesn't say, "Let me think about it. Clean it up a little bit and do better for a little while. Then I'll forgive you." We might act that way, but it's not how God forgives. He forgives us immediately.

Next, he forgives completely. When he's done with us, there isn't any residue of our sin left because he's wiped it completely away. You know how if your dishwasher's not working right sometimes it leaves bits of food on all the glasses and plates? You have to get it fixed and run the load of dishes through again. God forgives us the first time and doesn't leave any trace of our sins clinging to us. He forgives completely. The Bible says that he remembers our sins no more. *You* may still be worrying about what you did back in 2003, but God has moved beyond that.

Finally, he forgives us freely. Sometimes we think that his forgiveness is conditional based on what we do, but it's not. We can't do anything to earn it. It's free because Jesus paid the price completely when he died on the cross. He didn't go through all the pain and suffering of dying on the cross so that he could partially pay for our sins. No, he did it all, taking your sin and my sin on the cross. He took the punishment we deserved and paid our debt in full.

Seventy Times Seven

If we haven't received God's forgiveness fully and we don't feel forgiven, it's going to be hard to forgive others. It's difficult to give others what we haven't accepted in our own lives. So many people, even Christians, walk around with a cloud of guilt over their lives, carrying so much shame and condemnation. They're not living in a place of freedom because they don't truly understand that God has set them free and forgiven them. A key to a thriving life is understanding the incredible gift of full forgiveness that's made available to us through a relationship with God.

Jesus told us, "Freely you have received, freely give" (Matt. 10:8). So what we see is that we have to first come to God and embrace his forgiveness in our lives, and then we need to turn around and release it to others. Jesus instructed us to first pray, "Forgive us our debts" and then to pray, "as we also have forgiven our debtors." There's a link between the forgiveness we release and the forgiveness we receive.

I picture forgiveness as a continuous flow and we're its conduits. God's forgiveness is able to flow into my life, provided forgiveness is flowing out of me to those in my life who have wronged me. If we stop forgiving, the cycle and the flow get jammed up. We have to be willing to release forgiveness so that we can receive it. "Be kind and compassionate to one another, forgiving each other, just as in Christ God forgave you" (Eph. 4:32).

When we truly understand and embrace that we've been forgiven, it's so much easier to release people and to have compassion on people. Almost immediately after sharing the Lord's Prayer, Jesus said, "For if you forgive men when they sin against you, your heavenly Father will also forgive you. But if you do not forgive men their sins, your Father will not forgive your sins" (Matt. 6:14–15).

Wow. That's a pretty heavy statement. Jesus has just talked about forgiveness in the Lord's Prayer and now just a few verses later he goes back to the subject again, as if to re-emphasize the importance of it. Obviously, he was serious about this business of forgiveness. If we want to receive the forgiveness God has for us, then we must release forgiveness to the people in our world who need it. How we treat others. in this area of forgiveness affects what comes back into our own lives.

Jesus illustrates this in his response to Peter when he asked him how many times he had to forgive someone. It's like Peter asking, "Is seven times enough? Can I stop forgiving someone after that?" (see Matt. 18:21). I love Peter because he asks the questions everyone thinks about but is usually afraid to ask.

Jesus answers, "Not seven times . . . but seventy times seven!" (Matt. 18:22 NLT). Not exactly what Peter had in mind. Jesus was basically saying, "Stop counting how many times someone hurts you and just forgive—every time."

The need for forgiveness doesn't run out. Like our daily bread, it's an ongoing need in our lives. The great news is that God's capacity to forgive doesn't run out, and ours shouldn't either. To make his point really clear, Jesus shares a story.

He tells about a man who owed the king a huge sum of money, millions of dollars in today's terms. The man couldn't pay, so the king ordered him and his family and everything they owned to be sold to make payment for his debt. The man begged the king for mercy, and filled with compassion, the king released the man. He forgave him and canceled all his debt.

But here's the kicker. On the way out, the same man ran into someone who owed him money, about a month or two's wages. So our guy gets in his face and demands payment. When he finds out the man is unable to pay, he has him thrown in prison. Can you believe it? The same guy who was just given his life back by the king is unable to forgive someone for a much smaller amount.

But how often we do the same! We forget how much God has forgiven us when it's our turn to forgive others. In the story, the king hears what the man has done, gets angry, and throws him in jail until he can pay the debt. The man's lack of forgiveness to his peer limited his ability to truly receive and walk in the forgiveness he had been granted by the king. Jesus concludes, "So also My heavenly Father will deal with every one of you if you do not freely forgive your brother from your heart his offenses" (Matt. 18:35 AMP).

God isn't playing around when it comes to the issue of forgiveness. It *will* negatively impact our lives if we fail to forgive. When someone hurts us, if we don't forgive them from the heart—true, honest forgiveness that completely releases them—then we are sowing bad seeds, setting ourselves up to receive the same in return, and disrupting the flow of God's forgiveness in our lives.

We will all need forgiveness from somebody at some point. We can't expect the people in our world to forgive us if we are unwilling to forgive them. It's a two-way street. To keep making progress, maintain healthy relationships, and stay in a good flow with God so that nothing blocks our relationship with him, we must release the kind of forgiveness that Jesus gives us, the kind that's instant, complete, and free.

If there's someone in your life you need to forgive, I encourage you to do it today—don't wait. Your feelings may not change overnight, but forgiveness is a choice you make, not a feeling. Forgiveness isn't always easy, but it's the standard God's Word holds us to, and it's part of God's prescription for a healthy, happy life.

14

Locked In

The weak can never forgive. Forgiveness is
the attribute of the strong.

Mahatma Gandhi

Recently, Nancy Alcorn, the founder of Mercy Ministries, invited Leslie and me to visit their headquarters in Nashville. Nancy has been a friend of ours for several years and has an incredible heart for helping girls who are hurting. After working in a juvenile correctional facility for many years, she founded Mercy Ministries, and today, decades later, thousands of girls around the world have found hope and healing thanks to her incredible vision and the team at Mercy Ministries.

Mercy provides a free-of-charge, voluntary, faith-based residential program that serves young women who are facing life-controlling issues such as eating disorders, self-harm, drug and alcohol addictions, depression, and unplanned pregnancy. Mercy also serves young women who have been physically and sexually abused, including victims of sex trafficking. The girls stay in a beautiful group home, in an environment where they can find healing and restoration as they experience God's unconditional love, forgiveness, and life-transforming power.

Nancy asked me to speak at a staff meeting but also to address the girls. As I was praying and preparing my message for the girls in the home, I felt like God wanted me to speak on forgiveness. I knew it wouldn't necessarily be the easiest or most comfortable subject to bring up in a room full of hurting young women, many of whom had encountered abuse at the hands of people they trusted the most—mothers and fathers, siblings, and other loved ones. But I felt pretty certain God was leading me to do it, so I continued preparing to speak on the subject.

When the time came and I stood before them, I could see remnants of their stories in their eyes. Many of their faces carried the pain, the hurt, the anger, the confusion, and the lack of trust they were feeling inside. Some of them carried the scars on the outside as well. These girls had been through a lot, and I could tell that many of them had their defenses up.

When I had sensed God's leading to speak about forgiveness, I had said yes, but once I stood in front of them, it was a whole different ball game. I realized that I was about to ask some of them to do the seemingly impossible—to forgive the people who had shattered their worlds and made their lives a living nightmare.

After I finished speaking, the question and answer time quickly became intense. The kinds of things these girls had been through were beyond belief. Yet as we concluded our conversation about forgiveness, many of them were weeping, and it was clear that God was moving in their hearts in a powerful way. It was amazing to see the Holy Spirit start a significant work that day that took these young women one step farther on the road to freedom as they began to release hurts and unforgiveness they'd held on to for so long.

Living Proof

The testimonies of so many girls at Mercy Ministries are evidence that when we forgive, God empowers us to move forward and break free. When they share their stories, there's a constant theme: "Forgiveness helped set me free." They are living, breathing proof that forgiveness has the power to unlock our hearts and set us free. It's one of the key principles of the ministry, and I'm convinced it's one of the reasons so many girls there experience healing.

Whether or not they've experienced something as difficult as many of the girls at Mercy Ministries have, a great number of people struggle with forgiveness. In virtually every relationship in every area of our lives, we must learn to choose and practice forgiveness. Maybe it's an up-close and deeply personal offense experienced with your spouse. Perhaps it's the hurt that comes from a family member's sarcastic remarks.

Whether an offense is large or small, we are constantly faced with the choice to forgive. I have seen many people suffer a tragedy that required forgiveness, and they just couldn't bring themselves to forgive. As a result, they find themselves imprisoned by the hurt, stuck in the exact same place ten, fifteen, twenty years later. They're frozen in time, ongoing victims of what happened in the past, unwilling to or unaware of how to move forward. However, if we understand that we have the power to choose forgiveness, we have the key to unlock our prison cells and be free.

Bait and Switch

One of my favorite insights on forgiveness is found in the book of Proverbs, which tells us, "An offended brother is more unyielding than a fortified city, and disputes are like the barred gates of a citadel" (Prov. 18:19). This verse provides us with a dramatic picture that can help us understand the devastation of unforgiveness.

The Hebrew language is a very picturesque language. While in English we translate a word with one word, in Hebrew it could take an entire paragraph to describe a word's meaning. That's the case with the word *offended*.

The word *offended* here carries the image of an animal trap. When an animal smells the food, wanders into the trap, and grabs the bait, the door of the trap shuts and the animal is locked inside. This is the picture of being offended. This is what happens when we hold unforgiveness in our hearts. It locks us in. It traps us.

Offense is the bait. Someone says something harsh, and we get hurt. Emotions and thoughts rise up, and unforgiveness lures us in. The more we think about how wrong they were, the harder it is to resist. So we step into the trap and bam! The trapdoor slams down, and we're locked in—we're stuck. A lack of forgiveness keeps us imprisoned in the hurt from a moment, an event, or a relationship in the past. When someone does something to hurt us and we choose not to release that wound or release that person, then our lives move into lockdown mode.

Unforgiveness is like a cord tied around our hearts, wound tightly around the center of our lives, that leads back to that person and that situation. It keeps us tethered to something that's long been over. Many times the only thing that's keeping the situation alive is the bitterness and unforgiveness in our hearts. Often the person who hurt us has moved on, but we're still hanging on to the pain. It consumes the present and obscures the future.

Gardening Tool

I've noticed a pattern in my life, and I think it's true with all of us. Something happens or someone says something. It may be true or it may not be true. It may be our fault or we may be totally innocent. They may intend to hurt us or they may be totally oblivious. That action, that word, or that painful situation becomes a seed sown in the soil of our hearts. If we don't deal with it immediately and pull the seed out, it will bloom into a weed garden of pain and problems.

This is why the Bible tells us to guard our hearts with all diligence—because out of our hearts flow the issues of life. When we make a habit of maintaining our hearts and weeding out any seeds of offense, we keep our hearts healthy, full of life, and able to produce good fruit. "Love prospers when a fault is forgiven, but dwelling on it separates close friends" (Prov. 17:9 NLT). When we stop dwelling on an offense, we set ourselves up for good things, like love and peace, to grow and prosper. If we don't pull out a seed before it takes root, then we'll keep remembering what happened and thinking about it. We'll go back and read that email again. We'll listen to that voice mail again. We'll ask our friend, "Did he really say that?" And each time we go over it, we're watering that dangerous seed and planting it deeper in the soil of our hearts.

The best thing to do is short-circuit the process before the seed can sprout and put down roots into the soil of our hearts. I have a habit that I've established in my own life. Each night, before I go to sleep, I take a few moments to deal with anything in my heart that may be bothering me from the day. It's something I've implemented to keep those little seeds of offense from taking root and growing into something bigger. If we don't deal with them right away, they can progress into what the Bible calls a root of bitterness or a root of resentment. Eventually, those roots can start to overwhelm our souls.

Forgiveness is a gift we give ourselves, not the other person. We avoid being contaminated with negative things that steal our energy and resources. It's amazing the peace and strength that come into our lives when we choose to keep the soil of our hearts free from seeds of offense and bitterness. Forgiveness is the ultimate gardening tool, and using it regularly keeps our lives healthy, strong, and thriving.

Proceed with Wisdom

Forgiveness is a subject that gets people at the core. I know there's a chance that even as you are reading this there is a situation in your life that feels very complicated. You may have many unresolved questions in your mind about how forgiveness plays out practically speaking. When I talk about forgiveness, I always try to clear up some misconceptions about forgiveness because of the nature of the circumstances people are facing.

First, it's important to understand that there's a crucial difference between forgiveness and trust. Often when I've met with people and counseled them, I've found that they want to forgive but feel they can't because they believe doing so will reopen the wound. The offender will only hurt them again. But forgiveness is not the same as trust. You can, and must, forgive people who have hurt you, but that doesn't mean you automatically give them your trust again.

Sometimes there is abuse in relationships or other offenses that leave scars. The harmful actions were not God's plan or intention, but he can redeem those injuries in your life and restore you. You must forgive that person in order to release yourself, but that does not mean you subject yourself to their ability to harm or abuse you again. God's wisdom would caution us to protect our hearts from further injury. We must guard our hearts and be wise in determining how relationships should proceed.

Second, we must realize that forgiveness does not minimize the severity of the offense. When you forgive someone, you're not saying, "Oh, it was no big deal." Indeed, it may be a huge deal, which makes your forgiveness all the more necessary for your own healing. Even though you've forgiven

140

them, they still need to earn back your trust. Trust involves a consistent track record of responsible, committed, healthy behavior. When that trust is broken, we must choose forgiveness. But broken trust must be rebuilt, brick by brick, day by day, action by action.

Some people mistakenly believe that forgiveness allows the other person to continue on in how they are behaving. One man I counseled once said to me, "If I forgive them, then I have to accept them back just the way they are and allow them to continue to hurt me." No, you don't. Forgiveness is not the same as restoration. Forgiveness is what you do if you're offended. But if the relationship is going to be restored, then the person who has done wrong has to do three things: repent, make restitution where possible, and rebuild trust. I think it's worth saying that not all relationships should be restored. The best thing for you may be to move on, allow God to heal you, and trust that in time he'll bring new relationships that are good for you. Get some good counsel from wise, godly people who love you and commit to making choices that will allow you to move forward into health and wholeness.

When we forgive people, we release ourselves. The door of the trap opens up, and we can begin to find freedom. When we're standing in a weed garden of bitterness that's in full bloom, it's difficult to imagine life any other way. But true forgiveness uproots those weeds of bitterness and restores us to a place where we can experience life as God intended it—full of freedom, joy, and wholeness. We can step out of our self-imposed prisons and breathe fresh air again.

However, there's no way we can have that freedom if we're locked in the trap of unforgiveness. I can't begin to know all of the difficult situations or the pain you've experienced—some of them too deep and excruciating even to talk about without great difficulty. But I do know one thing. No matter how painful the wound or how long you've been living with it, God is powerful enough to give you the strength you need to release the people who have hurt you. His power is enough. His grace is enough. His strength is enough. You can be free from the trap of unforgiveness.

We can step out of the trap that's kept us contained and limited, or we can choose to stay locked in. Unlock the door and step outside the trap so you can move on with your life and God's plan for you. Choose to forgive.

15

Locked Up

Forgiveness is the key that unlocks the door
of resentment and the handcuffs of hate.

William Arthur Ward

Several years ago, I experienced a loss so devastating that it
brought life grinding to a halt. Part of its power was the element of surprise. We were celebrating because we had just
moved into a new facility for our church. No more renting a
place where we had to set up and take down everything before
and after the services each week. It felt like our hard work
was paying off, and we were finally gaining some momentum
in our lives and in our ministry.

On Saturday I was at the church, unpacking my office and
getting everything ready for the weekend. Before I could finish working, Leslie called and told me that she and the kids
were fine but to come home immediately. I went into high-
alert mode and knew something was terribly wrong. She'd
held herself together and gotten the kids settled watching a

TV show. When I arrived, she motioned for me to go into the bedroom.

"What's wrong? What's going on?" I asked.

Starting to cry, she choked out, "It's your dad—he's gone."

I was shocked. Frozen. Completely numb. In fact, I was having trouble processing the news. Surely there was some mistake—this wasn't possible. Leslie told me my dad had been out mowing his lawn like he did every Saturday and had suffered a stroke that ended his life.

The moment was surreal. I really couldn't wrap my mind around the fact that my dad's life could have ended so suddenly. How was this possible?

I immediately got on a plane to Baton Rouge so I could be with my mom and get funeral arrangements made. It was a whirlwind. I didn't give myself much time to grieve or mourn but instead tried to focus on being strong for my mom and sisters. We had about three days to get everything arranged for the memorial service. With so many details that needed to be taken care of, I had no choice but to press through, but the responsibility of arranging the memorial service weighed on me.

My father was very respected in his profession, and several hundred people were at the memorial service. There were former students from his decades of teaching at LSU, staff and faculty, as well as top officials and team members from the Center for Disease Control and other agencies. My father had touched many lives, and it was no small gathering.

Working through the loss of my dad was tough enough, but performing a memorial service in the presence of so many important and influential individuals added even more mental and emotional pressure. I really wanted to make it a service that would honor my dad, and in the end our family agreed we had achieved that. I was so thankful that I was able to be a part of it, but the process of planning and performing the service took it out of me.

After the memorial service in Baton Rouge, my family flew to Wisconsin, where my dad was originally from, to have a service with the rest of our relatives. My mom was having a really hard time. She was unable to shake the feeling that somehow my dad's death could have been prevented. She told me that a few weeks prior my dad hadn't been feeling quite like himself and had gone to the doctor. But as far as we knew, the doctor hadn't found anything to be concerned about and had sent him on his way. I tried to reassure her and reminded her that dwelling on it wouldn't help.

And I thought I really believed it myself, until something kind of snapped inside me. I'll never forget a particular moment sitting in the service in Wisconsin. I had asked my mom if the pastor in Wisconsin could do the service. I just wanted a chance to grieve the loss of my father. So there I sat, looking out at the beautiful cemetery, listening to this meek, mild-mannered pastor who sounded so kind and so gentle. But inside me, something started to churn. My mind was flooded with doubts and questions, and all kinds of emotions started rising up inside me.

I started thinking, *This can't be happening—my dad can't be dead. My kids will never get to know him . . . spend time with him . . . hear all his stories. If only the doctor had been more thorough, my dad might still be alive. I just can't believe he's gone. It wasn't supposed to turn out this way.*

The Tipping Point

All these thoughts began racing through my mind, and I began traveling down a dark road. I quickly stopped myself. I had to pull myself out of it. I told myself, *You cannot have these thoughts. You cannot start thinking like that. You cannot go down that road—it's not worth it. You have to let go. God is in charge here, not that doctor or anyone else.*

That was a pivotal moment for me, a tipping point. I was at the brink of unforgiveness and could have easily slipped over the edge into a very dark place. I felt it happening, and if

I had not stopped myself right then and there, I am confident that my feelings could have impacted my life and the lives of those around me in many ways.

I had started to lock up, to freeze up inside. I went from giving the benefit of the doubt to somehow wanting to blame the doctor or someone else for my dad's death. In the last chapter, we talked about how unforgiveness can keep us locked *in*, but it will also keep us locked *up*.

When we're locked up, we become brittle and unwilling to yield. For a brief moment at my dad's memorial service in Wisconsin, my heart started down the path of becoming hard and unyielding. I started thinking in a way that ultimately would have taken me in a negative direction. I wasn't handling my emotions well, and I started to embrace unforgiveness, resentment, and blame. I started to build walls around my heart and shut down.

When we're locked up, the walls we've built start to cut us off from the outside world. Nothing can go in or out, and we find ourselves in a dangerous position as a result. Anytime there's supposed to be a flow and the channel gets blocked, there's a problem. Without a flow or current to replenish its supply, a body of water grows stagnant and smells bad. If a person can't get oxygen in and carbon dioxide out, eventually they die. If a vein or artery gets clogged, we can go into cardiac arrest.

When we're locked up and the right things can't get in and the wrong things can't get out, it's only a matter of time before major problems emerge. We cannot afford to live with unforgiveness. We just can't. It will hurt us spiritually. It will hurt us emotionally and relationally. It will even impact us physically.

Stubborn as a Mule

One of the most significant repercussions of being hard and unyielding, or being locked up from unforgiveness, is that it cuts off the flow of God's work in our lives. When we're holding on to unforgiveness, it's harder to discern God's leading or sense his presence in our lives. Being stubborn or unyielding, especially when it comes to forgiving people, can leave us feeling confused and unsure what to do next. Or worse yet, maybe we sense the direction God is leading us in but we choose to ignore it. Sometimes we know what's right, but we choose not to obey because we are being stubborn. We're mad and hurting, and we don't want to budge.

But to put it simply, God tells us to forgive, and if we don't, it's sin. There's no way around it. Choosing to be stubborn and do things our own way, knowing we're going against the leading and direction of God, is a sure way to stop the flow of his blessing and work in our lives.

"The LORD says, 'I will guide you along the best pathway for your life. I will advise you and watch over you. Do not be like a senseless horse or mule that needs a bit and bridle to keep it under control'" (Ps. 32:8–9 NLT). Have you ever tried to get a stubborn animal to go in a certain direction only to have it refuse to budge? I've seen it happen with horses, with donkeys, with goats, even with dogs. Someone is tugging or pushing, shoving or dragging, and that animal has dug in and isn't moving!

You've heard the expression that someone is being "as stubborn as a mule" when they are being exceptionally hardheaded. The same is true of us when we lock up and refuse to follow God's guidance. We not only lose what God has ahead for us but also lose our sense of the present moment. We get stuck in the past, in the what-ifs and if-onlys of life. God wants to lead us through the pain to the other side, but we must stop being stubborn and unwilling to forgive. In Jeremiah 7:23–24, the Bible tells us that the Israelites' stubborn hearts and their refusal to obey God caused them to go "backward and not forward."

Obedience moves us forward. Disobedience causes us to go backward and moves us outside the covering of God's grace and protection. Regarding forgiveness, Matthew 6:15 in the Message says, "If you refuse to do your part, you cut yourself off from God's part."

Posted: Keep Out

Unforgiveness also locks us up emotionally and relationally. We begin to put up walls and distance ourselves, leading us into isolation. Many times this is a defense mechanism, a reaction to hurt and an attempt to protect ourselves. Some of this happens naturally, and we need to take time to work through hurts we experience in a healthy way. But if we're not careful and we don't manage our feelings and emotions well, we can slip into isolation.

We go from healthy boundaries and caution in forming friendships to shutting people out of our lives completely. We end up emotionally disconnected with only surface relationships, and even those are dominated by insecurity, fear, skepticism, resentment, and oversensitivity. We put up walls. Then over time we put locks on the doors so nobody can get in and blinds on the windows so nobody can see in. Before we know it, there are KEEP OUT signs plastered all over our lives.

Sometimes we drive people away with angry and harsh words. Sometimes we have an inability to commit to a relationship or to trust someone. Sometimes we just get tough and send out the vibe, "Don't mess with me—I'm fine on my own. I don't need anyone." But this is not what God intended. The Bible warns us about becoming isolated: "A man who isolates himself seeks his own desire; he rages against all wise judgment" (Prov. 18:1 NKJV).

We aren't setting ourselves up for success in life when we isolate ourselves. God created us to be in healthy, life-giving relationships. When we have people in our lives, we're able to accomplish more and we have someone to help us through life's rough patches. Good relationships encourage us and help us become better people.

Don't allow unforgiveness to isolate you. God didn't create you to walk through life alone. If you're hurting because someone has wronged you and you don't feel like you can be healed and have a close relationship again, I want to let you know that you can. God can heal you emotionally, and he can set you free from the pain. You don't have to live your life feeling crippled and damaged in your emotions. You are not damaged goods. God can restore you, heal you, and set you free. He can make you new.

Truth Decay

Unforgiveness can also eat us up from the inside out. It can affect us mentally. We play the same situation over and over in our heads, and with each repeated viewing we become angrier, more hurt, and more obsessed with our painful loss and its injustice.

We've already touched on the fact that unforgiveness poisons our emotions. As our thoughts remain stagnant and polluted by bitterness, our emotions follow suit. We get riled up, and the more we allow those feelings to dominate us, the more they fuel themselves and become stronger. We begin to form habits in our minds and emotions on how we deal with certain people and certain situations—learned responses that become our default setting.

We become angry, we become depressed, we become insecure, we become cynical, we become skeptical, or sometimes we just shut down emotionally and become numb. Our emotional problems don't affect just us; they affect the people around us—our spouses, our kids, our friends, and the people we work with. We need to get control of our emotions and not let them be in the driver's seat. We can't live by how we feel.

Finally, unforgiveness can affect us physically. Billy Graham said the he believed that 75 percent of patients in hospitals would be made whole if they would forgive.[1] And science seems to agree. Doctors have researched the effects of unforgiveness, and the toll it takes on our bodies is staggering. Consider these findings:

- People who are more forgiving report fewer health problems. In addition, learning to forgive may reduce feelings of hostility, a proven risk factor for heart disease.
- People who blame other people for their troubles have a higher incidence of illnesses such as cardiovascular disease and cancer.
- People who harbor resentment and refuse to forgive show negative changes in blood pressure, muscle tension, and immune response.[2]

The destructive results are undeniable. Unforgiveness causes decay and damage within us. The most powerful things we can do are take inventory of our lives, take responsibility for unlocking the areas in our hearts where resentment has lodged, and commit to following God's guidance. When we take responsibility for our hearts, our emotions, and the care of our souls, we close the door on a victim mentality and take one step closer to healing and wholeness.

Don't allow unforgiveness to rob you of the momentum God wants you to have in your life. Forgive today and choose not to live another day locked up in unforgiveness.

16

Locked Out

Resentment is like taking poison and waiting
for the other person to die.

Malachy McCourt

I grew up as the youngest of four with three older sisters. My
sisters and I enjoyed one of those love-hate relationships that
most siblings experience while growing up. We would argue
and tease one another, call one another names, and see who
could aggravate one another the most. One Saturday when I
was around twelve, our parents left us home alone, assuming
that my older sisters were more than able to handle things.
Oh, they handled things all right!

Knowing that our folks would be gone until late afternoon,
my sisters took every opportunity to torment me that day.
After the usual messing around, they reached the pinnacle of
their sisterly abuse when they locked me out of our house.
They sent me outside to get the mail, and when I came back,
all the doors were locked. The front door wouldn't budge,

151

and the garage door was locked tight, which left only the door on the side, the one we called the "den door" because it opened directly into our family room.

This door had several panes of glass, and what did I find when I turned the corner of the house? Not only was this door locked too, but my sisters were peering at me through the window, laughing their heads off at my annoyance. My sister Patty, who may have loved teasing me the most, even stuck her face up against the glass and made a face at me. That was the last straw. Without even thinking about what I was doing, I swung my fist at her—and it went *through* the glass!

Fortunately, I didn't cut myself very badly. And the shocked look on my sisters' faces was almost worth it. We immediately went into scramble mode, cleaning up the glass, taping some cardboard over the window, and thinking about the story we'd tell Mom and Dad. In a matter of moments, we went from being intense enemies to being united allies who knew we'd messed up. Our parents gave all of us consequences, and I remember going with my dad to the hardware store to purchase a pane of glass with my own money to replace the one I'd broken. Needless to say, it was a long time—at least another week—before my sisters and I got into it again.

Picking the Lock

If you've ever been locked out of your house or car, then you know it's no fun. It's frustrating, annoying, and ridiculously unnecessary. When it happens, you feel angry, impatient, and anxious. Instead of being able to get into a familiar and desired place, you're stuck on the outside. When you're locked out, you aren't able to be in the place you want to be.

As we've discovered in this section, forgiveness is a powerful locksmith. When Jesus taught us to pray, "Forgive us our debts as we forgive our debtors," he knew he was giving us a key to freedom. Consider again this verse in Proverbs: "An offended brother is more unyielding than a fortified city, and disputes are like the barred gates of a citadel" (18:19).

As we've seen in Scripture, unforgiveness can keep us locked *in*, as if we're in a cage or a trap, and it can also keep us locked *up*, rigid and immobilized. In this verse, we find one more reason to forgive: Unforgiveness can keep us locked out.

A city with "barred gates" has reinforced its entry points so well that no one can get in. That's what unforgiveness does to us. It builds heavy reinforcements on the gates to our future that prevent us from entering. It compromises our ability to see clearly. When we're constantly looking through the lens of unforgiveness, everything we see is dark and discolored. It's hard to picture the bright future God has for us when we're viewing life through bitterness. It's hard to keep our dreams before us when we're always looking over our shoulder at the past. If we don't practice the power of forgiveness, we will remain locked out of our future.

The Party's Over

One of the greatest stories in the Bible is one that may be familiar to you. It's the story of two sons and a father. They were obviously wealthy people and likely had a lot of sheep, cattle, and goats. One day, the youngest son went to his father and said, "I'd like my inheritance. I want it all right now so I can go. I've had enough of this."

So the father, with grace and generosity, gave his younger son all of his inheritance. Keep in mind the great insult he'd just experienced, because by asking for his inheritance while his father was still alive, the younger son was basically saying, "I wish you were dead. Since you're not, though, give me the money right now that's going to be mine." Not exactly the way to honor your father and show gratitude for all he's given you.

The younger son took his lump sum legacy and had the time of his life. The Bible says that sin is pleasant for a season. Why would we be tempted to sin if it didn't feel good, at least at the beginning? Until the consequences set in, indulgence feels good, and most people enjoy pursuing the things they crave in the moment. The younger son suddenly became a big spender and enjoyed attracting attention. He had all the fun he could have—partying with his newfound friends and socializing with the ladies.

But suddenly, he didn't have any money. Suddenly his new buddies and gold-digging girlfriends disappeared. He quickly discerned: no money = no friends = no partying. So our party boy had to get himself a job, and the only one he could find seemed like poetic justice: working with pigs.

He fell from being on top of the world to looking up at it from ground level. He took such a big fall that he found himself eating the same food he was feeding the pigs. Definitely not where he had planned to be when he had left his father's house all those months before. But finally he came around and realized something crucial to getting unstuck from his current situation. He realized how wrong he'd been and the disgrace he'd caused his father. He thought to himself, *The people who work for my dad have it better than this. I don't deserve to be considered my father's son anymore, but I'm going to go home and ask him if he'll take me in and let me work as a servant.* So he went home.

The Bible says that the father saw him while he was still a long way off. The father had been watching and waiting for him to return. He didn't go back inside the house and slam the door. He didn't yell out, "I told you so!" He simply ran to meet his son. This is a picture of the love God has for us and the forgiveness he extends to us.

The father ran to his son who had been lost and embraced him. He started calling for special gifts that represented honor and celebration. This over-the-top generous dad said, "Bring some shoes for his feet and a robe for his back. Bring a ring for his finger." He told the servants to kill the fattened calf (Luke 15:22–23). This kind of celebration was practically unheard of—especially for someone who had sinned against his father as the younger son had done. But now all the younger son could do was marvel at the grace and forgiveness his dad was showing him.

Not So Brotherly Love

But there was another son, and he wasn't in a party mood. He didn't like what he heard or what he saw. He couldn't believe his dad was going overboard to welcome home his loser of a brother. Had their dad lost his mind? Really, the fattened calf? A party? The older son struggled with the fact that the father could forgive his brother instantly, completely, and freely.

The older son couldn't understand how someone who had done what his brother had done could be celebrated. Soon his lack of understanding made it clear that he himself could not forgive his brother—or his father now for that matter. We're told, "The older brother became angry and *refused to go in*" (Luke 15:28, emphasis mine). He locked himself out of the party.

Maybe the older son was angry because he knew that part of his inheritance would go to his younger brother now. He'd have less because his brother had blown his inheritance partying and making bad decisions. I imagine he was thinking, *It's not fair. He needs to be punished. I'm always the one who does the right thing, while he messes up. Now he gets rewarded, and I'm going to be the one who pays for it.*

Maybe there was some truth to the things he was thinking and validity to the things he was feeling. But the bottom line is, when we withhold forgiveness, we lock ourselves out of the party. We choose to miss out. The older brother listened to his feelings and made a choice that kept him out of what was available to him—things his father wanted him to be a part of. The same is true with us. When we choose unforgiveness and resentment, we inevitably make choices that lock us out of the good things God wants to give us.

So many opportunities for progress and happiness are wasted when we make poor choices due to our feelings. "Surely resentment destroys the fool, and jealousy kills the simple" (Job 5:2 NLT). The truth is that when our hearts are filled with anger and resentment, we tend to do foolish things. A classic episode of *The Three Stooges* comes to mind. Moe kept hitting Curly on the chest, so finally Curly said, "I'm going to get even with that guy!" He found a few sticks of dynamite and strapped them to his chest. Satisfied with his plan, he said, "Next time he slaps me, that'll teach him. He'll blow his hand off!"

Here's the thing: Resentment doesn't work. Unforgiveness doesn't work. Often we want to make people pay. We want to lash out and cause them pain because they caused us pain. And sometimes the way we behave can hurt them, but more than anything, unforgiveness and resentment hurt *us*.

Unlock Your Future

Unforgiveness, anger, resentment, and blame are all closely related and usually intertwined. We get hurt, feel angry, and choose unforgiveness, which produces resentment, causing us to blame someone else for our issues. I mentioned earlier that resentment is kind of like the residue that's left after the rage and anger subside. It's acidic and continues to eat away at us long after the event has passed. The older brother probably held a lot of resentment toward his brother and his father.

But whether we choose to hold on to resentment or let it go is a choice *we* make—no one else can make the choice for us. We alone are responsible. We have to decide, and the choice can't be dependent on how we feel.

Holocaust survivor Corrie ten Boom said, "Forgiveness is an act of the will, and the will can function regardless of the temperature of the heart."[1] Feelings are a terrible manager of our lives. We have to do the right thing, often in spite of, not because of, our feelings. We won't always feel like doing the right thing, but we must commit to doing it anyway.

We can't live with a victim mentality. "It's not fair," we tell ourselves over and over again. And you know—we're right. It's not fair. So much of this life is unfair. But we can't change the past, and we can't live there. Dwelling on the past will ruin our future. Choosing to hold on to unforgiveness is like the toddler who wants to keep sitting in a dirty diaper. "It's gross and it stinks, but it's warm and it's mine, so I'll keep it."

The older brother's anger and resentment kept him from the party, kept him from celebrating something amazing that happened that day in the life of his father and their family. Are you locked out of something great that God wants to do in your life? God may want you to see and enjoy something significant, but you're locked out because you are angry and full of unforgiveness. Unforgiveness could be the very thing that's keeping you from going in and taking hold of your future.

Forgiving others is one of the greatest secrets to getting unstuck. Your future depends on your ability to give forgiveness freely. Your marriage depends on it. Your wholeness depends on it. What do you need to let go of? Who in your world do you need to forgive and release? Let them go. Your life will be better for it. Let's remember to be good forgivers and good forgetters.

Maybe this prayer will help you get started. If there's someone you need to forgive, I encourage you to take that step right now. Let today be the day you start to walk into the future God has for you.

One step forward: Heavenly Father, I don't want to be held back by unforgiveness. Help me to be humble enough to release the things I've held on to. Heal the broken places and restore my heart. I choose to let go of my hurt and resentment. [If you have someone you need to forgive, I encourage you to pray specifically about that person right now and release them and the pain you've been carrying.] Allow me to use the key of forgiveness to unlock the door to my future so I can step into it with joy, freedom, and wholeness. Thank you that you always welcome me back home, just like the prodigal son's father did. Help me to do the same for others and to celebrate your grace not only in my life but also in theirs. In Jesus's name, amen.

PURSUIT

ALIGNING YOURSELF WITH GOD'S PLAN FOR YOUR LIFE

17

Where He Leads

Lead us not into temptation, but deliver us
from the evil one.

Matthew 6:13

As I shared with you earlier, Leslie and I moved to Africa to
be missionaries shortly after we got married. We loved it and
thought we might spend our whole lives there. But after about
three years, we began to get the feeling that we were supposed
to return home and start a church. So with the blessing of
our pastor, we returned to the States and embarked on our
new adventure.

I was fired up, and I couldn't wait to jump in and get
started. I had a vision for the church, and deep down in my
heart I knew that Leslie and I were supposed to devote our
lives to making a difference, to starting a church that would
reach people and rescue the hurting and broken. We didn't
waste any time getting started. After spending two weeks in
Baton Rouge with our families, we loaded a U-Haul with the
few possessions we owned and moved to Memphis.

I'll be honest. That first year was hard. Much harder than
we expected. We reached the second year . . . and it was still

hard. We were optimistic that the third year would bring the growth and momentum we were praying for and working to achieve. It didn't. Leslie and I knew that growth wouldn't come overnight, and we were prepared to work hard. We just didn't have any idea it would be *that* hard. The church wasn't growing the way I thought it would, and no matter what I did, we just couldn't seem to get anywhere near the picture I had in my heart. I was trying hard not to lose hope.

One Sunday we had a particularly discouraging service. Attendance was down, and everyone's energy felt especially low. I felt like no matter what I said throughout the service, people just stared at me from their seats. On the way home from church, I stopped to get some sandwiches. Leslie was usually putting Anna down for her nap about the time I'd get home, so I'd gotten in the habit of picking up the Sunday paper and looking through it while I ate. I'd check out the classifieds, looking at different jobs and imagining other career options. It was kind of an escape, a way for me to get away from the frustrations and discouragement that surrounded my current reality for a few minutes. As I was scanning through the classifieds that Sunday, my daydream was interrupted as Leslie came back into the kitchen.

"What are you doing?" she asked. The tone of her voice told me that it wasn't really a question. She knew exactly what I was doing. She was aware of some of the thoughts and feelings I'd been having and knew why I was looking at the classifieds. I was toying with the idea of quitting, and she was challenging me on it. Leslie looked at me for a long time and then said, "We're not quitting."

Never Give Up

My wife called me out, and I'm so glad she did. I don't give up easily, and I'm a pretty determined person. I'm not afraid of hard work, and I'm willing to do whatever is necessary to reach my goals. I had been fighting the temptation to give up for a long time and had been doing a pretty decent job resisting it. But it was getting tougher, especially on Sunday afternoons after a dismal service.

The temptations of those early years were strong. There was the temptation to compare myself to other people whom I viewed as more successful than me, the temptation to quit and move on to something new, the temptation to give up on the dream and settle for what we currently had. I was tempted to say, "Fine. I guess this is as good as it gets. I've done everything I can. I'm done trying." I was tempted to give up. And for a while I did.

I may not have quit on the outside, but I quit on the inside. I was just going through the motions. I let my faith and optimism wither into frustration, and fragments of apathy and cynicism began to creep in. Thankfully, that despondent season didn't last long. God reminded me of his presence, and we continued to keep at it, even in the tough times.

Today, I'm glad we didn't quit because I'm seeing the dreams in my heart become a reality. But there were plenty of tests, trials, and temptations along the way. And they almost took me off course. I almost got stuck—permanently.

Many of us face crossroads decisions every day. We're in a season in which nothing goes right, and it's tempting to give up, run the other way, or find relief in the wrong ways. These can be some of the most difficult times to keep moving forward. They are also some of the most defining moments in our lives. That's why Jesus instructs us to go to the Father and ask for his help when we are tempted or when we are walking through a challenging season.

Trials and Temptations

In the Lord's Prayer, Jesus prays, "Lead us not into temptation, but deliver us from the evil one" (Matt. 6:13). The word used for temptation here is *peirasmos*. It's a Greek word that has the root meaning "to test" or "to prove," and it can be used in two ways. It can be used to mean "trial," meaning a challenging season in which we are tested, or it can be used to mean "temptation," referring to something that is enticing us to do wrong.

First, it's important to realize Jesus isn't implying that God is the one who tempts us. James, the brother of Jesus, makes this clear: "And remember, when you are being tempted, do not say, 'God is tempting me.' God is never tempted to do wrong, and he never tempts anyone else. Temptation comes from our own desires, which entice us and drag us away. These desires give birth to sinful actions. And when sin is allowed to grow, it gives birth to death'" (James 1:13–15 NLT). He uses the same word for temptation, *peirasmos*. So we know very clearly that James was saying our temptations do not come from God.

Interestingly enough, James uses the same word, *peirasmos*, just a few verses prior when he talks about being tested. "Consider it pure joy, my brothers, whenever you face trials of many kinds, because you know that the testing of your faith develops perseverance" (James 1:2–3). Or consider how the Amplified Bible puts it: "Consider it wholly joyful, my brethren, whenever you are enveloped in or encounter trials of any sort or fall into various temptations. Be assured and understand that the trial and proving of your faith bring out endurance and steadfastness and patience."

In this part of the Lord's Prayer, Jesus is telling us that we should ask God to guard us and keep us safe in the midst of life's challenging seasons, whether we are being tempted and enticed by our own desires or are surrounded by a trial that tests our endurance. In either case—and many times the two seem to go together—these are both prime opportunities for us to get off track and lose momentum.

Let's think about each of these situations for a moment. A trial or a season of testing is a time when difficult circumstances come our way. Many times they are situations out of our control, situations unrelated to anything we've done.

They may include a parent with Alzheimer's, the loss of a loved one, a financial deal falling through, a child getting sick and needing ongoing care, a layoff due to downsizing. In each case, we end up bearing an enormous weight—physically, financially, emotionally, mentally, and spiritually.

Those are seasons that test us, our character, our commitment, and our faith. Such seasons are hard, and we don't know how things are going to work out when we're in the midst of them. Sometimes we feel like they are pushing us to the breaking point. Sometimes we get weary. We may feel like giving up.

We have to be careful in those moments and seasons to dig down deep and stay committed to the principles in God's Word. We can't allow ourselves to make bad decisions based on our feelings. We need to commit to keeping our spirit and soul healthy by sowing good seeds, even in difficult times. To resist temptation, we must speak the truth of God's Word over ourselves and our situations. We must choose to have a positive attitude even when we feel discouraged. We must remain committed to God and put action to our faith even in the most challenging of seasons.

According to James, trials actually help perfect and complete us. They strengthen the weak spots in our lives if we handle them correctly. These seasons of testing are increasing our capacity and making us better and stronger for things we'll face on the journey ahead.

James also tells us that we will face temptation that comes from our own desires. These desires can entice us and drag us off course. Desire is a longing or hoping for something. Desire is one of the strongest and most powerful drives a human being possesses. We often hear the word and associate it with things of a sexual nature, but desire is by no means limited to the sexual arena of our lives. Anything we want badly enough, anything we have strong emotions of longing or hoping for, reflects a desire. It could be for wealth, fame, significance, approval, to achieve a certain image or appearance, to find a spouse, or to have kids.

Certainly, our desires are not always bad. But even good desires, such as the desire to have a spouse or provide for our family, can turn into areas of temptation if we aren't careful. The devil knows how powerful desire is, and that's why he appeals to it. He knows how hard it can be to say no to ourselves, especially when our defenses are weakened by discouragement and exhaustion.

Whether or not we realize it, we're involved in a struggle that's larger than our immediate circumstances. The struggle we face is not just against other people or our own desires. The Bible tells us we are involved in a spiritual battle (Eph. 6:12). The devil has a plan for us; it is a plan for destruction and to rob us of a thriving life. Scripture tells us that he comes to kill, steal, and destroy (John 10:10). He's compared to "a roaring lion looking for someone to devour" (1 Peter 5:8).

We need to be aware of the devil and his ways so we can withstand his tricks and tactics in our lives. The devil's plan is to kill and destroy, but Christ came to give abundant life. We should not lose heart when we go through a difficult season. "In this world you will have trouble. But take heart! I have overcome the world" (John 16:33). Yes, we're in a spiritual fight, but God has already won.

Sometimes we may sense that God is working on a specific area through our struggles. Other times difficult things come our way and we can't necessarily identify a certain lesson God wants us to learn. Instead of asking "Why me?" we need to focus on navigating that situation well so it doesn't hold us up. We have to trust that God can take even things intended for evil and use them for good (Gen. 50:20).

Guard Duty

So how do we navigate challenges well and avoid getting stuck or off course?

The first way we prepare is by developing an awareness of our weaknesses and our enemy's ploys against us. We must be on our guard. We're told to "stay alert!" and "watch out!" so that we're not surprised by the ravenous lion who wants to devour us (1 Pet. 5:8). In other words, we can't get caught off guard, get slack, or be lazy. We have to stay at the top of our game spiritually so that we aren't in a position to get picked off by the devil.

In Africa, we went to the game reserves, and each time we saw that the lions and other hunting animals would pick on the stragglers, the animals who had wandered away from the herd or from their secure environment. Those lions would lie in wait until the perfect moment when a straggler was distracted. Then they would charge and attack viciously. Let me tell you, I've seen it firsthand, and it's intense. These weren't photo ops for tourists or commercials for *Animal Planet*. These were vicious, bloody attacks that reduced a living creature to a heap of fur and bones in a matter of minutes.

The same can happen to us if we start to relax in our spiritual lives. If we go off on our own and think we don't need a church home or that we don't need relationships of accountability, we're setting ourselves up as a prime target to be ambushed. In Mark 14:38, Jesus tells us, "Watch and pray so that you will not fall into temptation. The spirit is willing, but the body is weak." We each have different areas where we can be tempted. Whether it's lust, negativity, or insecurity, we have to know those areas where we tend to get tripped up. We must guard against them and keep the door closed to those things. We can't let the devil creep in and ambush us.

Next, we must exercise self-discipline. There's no way around it. Success in life requires us to exercise self-discipline, especially in seasons of testing, trials, and temptation. Part of unlocking our potential and moving forward in life is having the self-discipline to say no to the wrong things and yes to the right things. A lack of self-discipline can destroy even the greatest potential. We've got to be willing to delay grati-fication and not be controlled by our desires and emotions.

Finally, if we want to navigate challenging seasons well, we must press into God. Sometimes the last thing we feel like doing is exerting spiritual energy to draw close to God. When tough times come, we may feel the urge to withdraw from God, especially if we're dealing with feelings of frustration, disappointment, hurt, or anger toward him. But we've got to keep our hearts in check and never allow our feelings to foster bitterness and resentment. Even if it's the last thing we feel like doing, we must gather our strength and draw close to God during life's difficult seasons.

God loves us, and we can rely on the truth that he always has our best interests at heart. Staying close to God will help us make it through the challenges and temptations that we face so we can keep making progress and finish strong.

18

The Pursuit

It is not in the pursuit of happiness that
we find fulfillment, it is in the happiness of
pursuit.

Denis Waitley

Leslie and I grew up three blocks from each other and were in
the same kindergarten class. We went to the same elementary
school and hung out with the same pack of friends from our
neighborhood. We would even play together at recess. *Starsky
and Hutch* was the hot show back then, so my buddy and I
did our best impression of the two tough guys while she and
her friends watched and giggled.

In sixth grade, she went to a different middle school, but
we stayed connected by the group of friends we had in common, and we ended up at the same school for ninth grade.
And that's when it all changed. That was the first time I saw
her—I mean *really* saw her. She looked different to me suddenly, like more than just a friend, and I started thinking of
her in a whole new way.

Over the next few years, we remained friends and hung out together with our little group. I admired her, how she treated her friends, how she honored her parents, how she prepared for class—basically, how she lived her life. She was smart and thought for herself. She took care of herself and always looked nice in her button-down shirts with a perfect, color-coordinated bow in her hair. I was sold. She was the girl for me. I was determined that our friendship needed to move forward into something greater.

By the end of tenth grade, I finally got up the nerve to ask a friend to find out if she was interested in me. The response she gave him was something along these lines: "I mean, I like him, but . . . we're really good friends, and I don't want anything to ruin our friendship."

I decided I wasn't giving up. No "but" was going to stand in my way! I asked her out anyway and kept pressing her to give dating a chance. I always joke that I went to her and said, "Come on, baby! Let's take a risk. Let's push all the chips to the center of the table and sacrifice our friendship on the altar of romance." (Don't worry—I don't think I was suave or melodramatic enough to say that.) Whatever I did say worked, though, because she agreed to go on a real date with me.

At the beginning of eleventh grade, we went on our first date in none other than the legendary Ford Fairmont. I'd over-heard her say once that Grey Flannel was her favorite men's cologne, so I went out and bought some. Sure enough, she noticed and was impressed. We went to the Varsity Theater on the LSU campus, an amazing vintage theater where they showed old movies, and watched Alfred Hitchcock's *Vertigo*. If you've seen that classic film, then you know it doesn't have the happiest of endings. However, the date must not have been too bad because Leslie agreed to go out with me again.

That date was the start of an incredible adventure that eventually led to our engagement and marriage years later. Fast-forward over twenty years to the present, and our relationship is stronger and better than ever. It all started with my pursuit of her, and we continue to move forward today because we make it a priority to continue to pursue each other in our relationship.

Thrill of the Chase

Pursuit is a powerful force. It moves us from where we are to where we want to be. It helps us step into our future and, in many ways, helps shape that future. Usually in life, if we don't pursue something, it remains out of reach. Pursuit helps us close the distance between our current situation and the dream in our hearts. It takes the vision and the picture we see in our minds and helps make them a reality. Jesus told us to pray that God would "lead us" and "deliver us." And I'm confident that the way we experience his leading and deliverance is by pursuing him with our entire being.

The word *pursue* means "to chase, to hunt, to be occupied with." There's the idea of following, but there's also a sense of mission, an urgency and an intensity with purpose. We've acknowledged that in life there can and will be difficult seasons—times of testing, trials, and temptation. Pursuing God is key to staying on track as we fight through a challenging season, but it's also the starting point for achieving any kind of true success and significance in life. The goals we choose to pursue chart the course of our lives, revealing our priorities, our failures, and our accomplishments. *What* we pursue determines the direction our lives will take. *How* we pursue our goals determines the pace of our forward momentum.

When we pray for God to lead us and deliver us, we're asking for direction based on God's wisdom, for strength to withstand temptation and testing, and for God's protection to keep us safe.

However, in order for God to lead us and deliver us, we must be in step with him, following, pursuing him. "Come

171

close to God and He will come close to you" (James 4:8 AMP). It's important for us to know that he responds to our pursuit. He has already extended his love and his open arms to us, drawing us near, so the ball is in our court to take the next step and pursue him. As we pursue him, he responds.

Just Do It

So what does pursuit look like in our lives? There are three things we need to do. First, we must take initiative in our relationship with God. We've got to be willing to make a move. Sometimes it means taking a risk. We've got to have the motivation and the guts to *do* something. We've got to take action! Thinking isn't enough. Intentions aren't enough. Pursuing takes *action*.

One of the greatest examples of initiative can be found in three places in the Bible. A woman had a chronic medical condition that had kept her bleeding for twelve years. The Bible says, "She had suffered a great deal from many doctors" (Mark 5:26 NLT). She'd endured countless "treatments." She'd spent everything she had trying to find answers, but she had only gotten worse. Think of the turmoil she must have gone through both physically and emotionally for over a decade. But then she heard about Jesus. She thought to herself, *If I can only touch the edge of his garment . . .* As she touched it, Jesus felt power leave him, and she was healed. Jesus asked, "Who touched my robe?" "His disciples said to him, 'Look at this crowd pressing around you. How can you ask "Who touched me?"'" (Mark 5:30–31 NLT).

It was extremely crowded around Jesus. She wouldn't have had easy access to him. She had to press in and fight her way through the crowd to be able to touch Jesus's robe. She may have even had to get down on her hands and knees and crawl to be able to get to him. Clearly, she was determined.

She knew that Jesus held the answer to her problem, and she was set on getting close enough to touch him. The crowd didn't stop her, the risk of getting trampled didn't stop her, the possibility of failure didn't stop her. She saw an opportunity, and she went for it. And it changed her life. If she had failed to pursue Jesus, she would have missed out on a life-altering moment that literally transformed her from the inside out. Transformation takes place on the path of pursuit. Our lives are changed as we take initiative and pursue Jesus.

If you are not a person who takes initiative, you will not move forward very quickly. You will not experience all that God has for you. Being willing to take initiative is one of the greatest things we can do in life to build momentum. When I began to notice Leslie in a new way, I began devising plans, thinking of ways to be around her, to spend time with her. Ultimately, I went and said to her, "I think we'd be better together." I had to initiate. I had to take it upon myself to do something and be proactive. I had a vision of what our future together could look like, and that vision moved me to action.

In Hot Pursuit

The second thing we need to do is pursue God with passion. You've heard the phrase "in hot pursuit," right? There's some passion involved in the chase. We need to be fired up, to have some enthusiasm burning strong on the inside. We can't be complacent if we are going to be good pursuers. If we have a relationship with no passion or pursuit, it will usually come to an end and fizzle out. We can't base everything on how we feel, but passion is really not just about that.

Did you know that the word *passion* has been used through-out history to describe what Jesus went through on the cross? The word *passion* has its roots in a Latin word that means "to suffer" or "to endure." So many times we think passion is about love and feelings and excitement. But really it's more about being so committed to something that we're willing to see it through to the end because we believe in it and value it. Jesus loved passionately, and it made him willing to go to the cross, suffer, and die for us. Jesus was committed to pursuing his Father's plans and making a relationship with God available to us.

There may be times when we don't *feel* passion. That's the time we have to stir it up inside ourselves. Paul told Timothy to fan into flame the gift God had given him (2 Tim. 1:6–7). Timothy was pursuing the call of God on his life as a young pastor of a very large church, and Paul, his mentor, was letting him know that he needed to cultivate some passion.

On Purpose

Not only do we need to take initiative and pursue God with passion, but if we are going to be good pursuers, we also need to live with a purpose. Proverbs 29:18 tells us that without vision people perish (AMP).

Some people have enough motivation, but without purpose it can get misdirected. Purpose, or vision, keeps us on track. It gives us a lane to run in, parameters and boundaries. Otherwise, we can tend to be all over the map, going this direction one day and that direction the next. Passion can get us into trouble if we don't have a purpose to harness it and keep us pressing toward the right goal.

God created you *on* purpose *for* a purpose. Before you were even born, God knew you, and he knew the specific plans he had for you. Your life was not an accident. You are here for a reason. When you understand this, it changes how you live. You have something to run toward day after day, something to do and somewhere to go. If you are struggling with this issue of purpose, keep drawing near to God. Pray and ask him to help you in this area, then start doing something you are good at and find ways to help people.

We are all pursuing something, whether or not we realize it. Our core motivation behind the things we pursue usually comes down to what we perceive the payoff to be. We must ask ourselves not only what we're pursuing but also what we hope to gain from it.

Right now, what are you pursuing? More time or a moment's peace? The weekend? Success at work? Getting better at a skill or hobby? Maybe it's a relationship you're going after. Maybe you're pursuing a fitness or weight-loss goal or achieving a certain appearance.

It's important that we take time to ask ourselves these questions: *What am I moving toward? What's currently determining my steps? What is compelling me or driving me forward? What am I chasing?*

Deep inside each of us there is an emptiness we try to fill. Sometimes we end up chasing and pursuing the things— anything—we believe will fill the hole. At the core of our pursuit is a desire for satisfaction and happiness. God made us that way and put that desire there. We can't fill that emptiness on our own, so we go looking for ways to fill it. Doing so can lead us off the path of God's best and even into situations that can have serious consequences in our lives. Sometimes we can find temporary happiness and fulfillment, but in the end, the price is always greater than we bargained for.

One of the devil's greatest tricks to get us off track is tempting us with the thought that things other than God will satisfy the longing and desire inside. He knows that if we buy into that lie we'll never fulfill our God-given purpose. We won't be and do all God created us to.

The truth is this: There is nothing other than Jesus that can satisfy us fully. We have to pursue the right things so we don't end up somewhere we don't want to be. Physics tells us that if our golf swing is off by a fraction of a degree when we strike the ball, the ball will get more and more off track the farther it goes. What we pursue and how we pursue it determine where our lives will go.

There is nothing more important to pursue than Jesus. We have to know and believe at the core of our beings that our greatest satisfaction and happiness are found in knowing and experiencing Jesus for ourselves. If we pursue him first above all else and are fully focused on him and his kingdom, we will find the true fulfillment that our hearts are searching for.

19

Follow the Leader

The mark of a good leader is to know when
it's time to follow.

Susie Switzer

Before Leslie and I were married, I spent an entire summer
in Kenya with our pastor, Don Matheny. He and his wife,
Amy, have spent over thirty-five years as missionaries in Africa and are some of the most influential and significant
people in our lives. Over the years, we have learned so much
from them, and they've become great mentors and friends
to Leslie and me.

During that summer, I got to stay a few days on a remote
Muslim island off the coast of Kenya called Paté Island, where
Pastor Don had started an outreach several years earlier. He
would stay three weeks at a time, live in a tent, bring his own
food, and trek to remote villages on the island. He'd show the
Jesus film and tell the people about God. It was hard work,
and after years of reaching out to these people, Pastor Don

had seen a handful of men accept Jesus into their lives and establish a church, which was a miracle in this strict Muslim area.

I'd heard a lot of incredible stories about Pastor Don's work there, so when the opportunity presented itself, I was eager to see the remote island and meet the believers there—true heroes in my eyes.

For the first leg of the trip, I had to fly from Nairobi to Malindi, a city on the coast of the Indian Ocean. There I spent the night at the home of a rugged missionary who took me to the very end of the coast to catch a ferry to Lamu Island. From there, I'd have to take a bus to the other end of Lamu, where I'd meet a guide who would take me by yet another boat to Paté. I felt like I was part of the original *The Amazing Race*! My missionary host told me, "When that bus pulls up, run as fast as you can and get a seat. If you miss it, you'll have to wait a whole day to catch the next one."

As soon as the bus arrived, it was a mad dash to get on—no sense of order whatsoever. People were pushing, shoving, holding chickens that were flapping and squawking with feathers flying everywhere. Talk about culture shock. After all, I was just a nineteen-year-old kid from Baton Rouge!

When we made it to the other end of Lamu Island, my guide and I got something to eat and found a place to spend the night. The next morning we got an early start since, of course, there was only one boat a day from Lamu to Paté. Each leg of my journey was increasingly more remote and more exotic. I felt like I was Indiana Jones making his way through the small streets of an unfamiliar village with high walls and animals roaming everywhere.

The next day, I finally arrived on Paté Island and got the opportunity to preach at the church I'd heard so much about. My journey to get there gave me new insight into what it means to follow directions—and more important, to have a guide. I never would have made it without someone leading me every step of the way.

Finding Our Way

Just like I needed that guide to lead me and keep me safe while en route to my ultimate destination that morning, we need God to lead us on our journey through life. With this in mind, it's clear why Jesus tells us in the Lord's Prayer to ask God to lead and deliver us.

God doesn't want us to go through life feeling lost, wandering aimlessly, lacking direction. He doesn't want us stuck in place, fighting the same battles or going through the same old routine we've been going through for years. He wants to lead us each day, to give us fresh insight and direction that apply to what we're facing right now so that we can make good decisions.

God knows exactly where we are today and the situations we're facing, as well as what's ahead. He wants to give us a set of directions that will take us on the best route to get us to our destination. His desire to lead us couldn't be clearer throughout his Word: "I will guide you along the best pathway for your life. I will advise you and watch over you" (Ps. 32:8 NLT).

Life can get complicated, and there are times when we don't know what to do or where to go. Jesus told us to ask God to lead us because he never intended for us to have to navigate our paths alone. God is available to help us make good decisions and avoid potholes in life if only we will look to him for direction. We have to open our hearts, yield our plans, and follow God's guidance on a daily basis. There are three primary ways God leads us: through his Word, through his people, and through his voice in our hearts.

Follow the Light

When we refer to being led by God's Word, we're talking about finding guidance in the Bible. God's Word is the ultimate source of truth. It's our standard for what's right and wrong and the way we live our lives. It's the only source of guidance that's completely accurate, unchanging, and everlasting. The Bible says, "Heaven and earth will pass away, but [God's] words will never pass away" (Matt. 24:35).

The Bible is packed with practical wisdom for everyday life that sets us up to win. Scripture has an amazing number of verses about money, relationships, peace, overcoming bad habits, gaining wisdom, building inner strength to withstand challenges, and so much more. It addresses the practical things we think about, worry about, and deal with on a daily basis.

The Bible also has the supernatural power to change and strengthen us. God's Word brings insight into who God is and how we should relate to him. It is living and active, powerful like a two-edged sword. It is able to divide the soul from the spirit, meaning that it can help us discern our feelings from what is true about a situation in our lives.

Here's one of my favorite things about the Bible: It gives us direction and clarity. "Your word is a lamp to my feet and a light for my path" (Ps. 119:105). Sometimes we reach a place where life feels so dim and hazy, so obscured by all the choices, options, responsibilities, and relationships that pull at us. We need help prioritizing and sorting things out. We need to see clearly what we're doing and where we're going.

Remember my journey to Paté Island? Well, my return was just as long and cumbersome. In fact, it was a little tougher because I had gotten really sick from something I'd eaten, which meant hiking across the island for two hours wasn't easy. The fact that we had to get up at 4 a.m. to catch the one boat back at 7 a.m. didn't help either!

On top of it all, my guide warned me about the wild animals that could be hiding along our path. So here I was hiking for over two hours, sicker than a dog, and worrying about running into a lion in the dark. My guide helped, though, and said, "You'll see my flashlight ahead, but you'll need your own. You'll have to hold it right in front of you. You won't be able to see much, but you will be able to see your next couple of steps."

As my stomach rumbled and lurched, I clutched my little flashlight and prayed that someone had put brand-new batteries in it. That was a difficult trek to say the least, but my guide was right. In the darkness, I could see a couple of feet in front of me. That was enough, and I made it out safely.

This is the case with the Word of God. Sometimes we're afraid, we're not feeling well, there may be things out to get us, and there's darkness all around us, but the Word of God can illuminate the path right in front of us. We may not be able to see far, but all we need to see is the step right in front of us. And then the next. We just need to keep going, letting him show us where to take each step.

You've Got a Friend

In addition to his Word, God uses people to lead us. God puts people around us to help, strengthen, and teach us and at times even to provide direction.

The local church was intended to be the kind of place where people can be connected in loving, authentic relationships, where we can find people who can encourage us, challenge us, and speak into our lives. We don't open our lives to everybody, but there should be certain people who know us inside and out. They know our secrets, our fears, and our dreams, and they offer their support, their encouragement, and their prayers.

When we're frustrated at work by our boss's attempts to micromanage us, when we're worried about our finances, when we're hurting from losing a loved one, when we're struggling in our marriage, we need good people to love us and tell us the truth.

The Bible is filled with verses about the value of having wise counsel and seeking wisdom from those who are godly and mature. "Fools think their own way is right, but the wise listen to others" (Prov. 12:15 NLT). "Get all the advice and instruction you can, so you will be wise the rest of your life" (Prov. 19:20 NLT).

I'm so grateful I have certain people in my life who know me well and speak into my life. I wouldn't even think about making a big decision without talking to them and getting their advice and counsel. They help me see God's hand in my life, sense the next steps where he's leading me, and stay out of potential pitfalls on life's journey.

If you don't have good people around you who can speak wisdom into your situations, then you must make it a priority to find some. Think about the people in your life you know and trust. Is it time to take your relationship to the next level by letting them into your life in a more significant way? You may need to take some initiative, allow yourself to be vulnerable, and carve out some time in your busy schedule.

If we want the benefits of true, authentic relationships, we have to be able to share what's really taking place on the inside. Honest, healthy relationships and friendships help us move forward. They are a key way that we experience God's truth and guidance in our lives.

Can You Hear Me Now?

Finally, God still speaks to us today and leads us with his voice. One time my daughter Anna and I were riding in the car, and she asked how Leslie and I had known that God wanted us to move to Memphis. In my response, I mentioned something about God speaking to me. This prompted her to ask a question that most of us have considered at one point or another: "What does God's voice sound like?" Her question made me think because, of course, I hadn't heard a thundering, audible voice but rather a thought, a quiet knowing, a deep sense from within my heart. It was something I knew I hadn't come up with on my own.

"Well, it kinda sounded a little like my voice, only different." I don't know if that made sense to her, but it was the best way I could describe it in the moment, and actually, I've found that it's still one of the simplest ways that I can explain what it's like to hear God's voice.

Hearing God's voice can be an incredible and powerful experience that helps us tremendously. But I would also caution you to learn how to discern his voice within you because it can indeed sound a lot like your own. We could easily talk ourselves into believing it's God's voice when it's really our own, or we may do the opposite. We may write something off as our own thought or idea when God is really trying to speak to us. So we need to take care as we grow in our faith to develop a sensitivity, an ability to listen carefully and know the difference.

I think about the story of Samuel, the prophet, hearing God's voice as a young boy. Samuel lived and served in the house of God under the priest Eli. He was sleeping one night and heard someone call his name. He went straight to Eli and asked him why he'd called him. It was God, of course, speaking to Samuel, but he didn't realize it. The voice of God must have sounded a lot like Eli, his leader, or else it was the only voice he assumed could have been calling him in the night.

Either way, he went right to Eli, who said, "I didn't call you, go back to bed." It happened two more times, and then Eli realized what was going on. He told Samuel, "Go and lie down, and if he calls you, say, 'Speak, LORD, for your servant is listening'" (1 Sam. 3:9).

God was speaking to Samuel, but Samuel didn't realize it. Samuel needed the help of someone else to fully recognize the voice of God in his life. That's why it's so important to listen carefully and to be open to the voice of God, as well as the counsel of others. We need to check ourselves before we immediately jump to the conclusion, "Yep, God just spoke to me, so I'm doing it." We also don't want to be closed off and miss what God is trying to get across to us. It's important that we be quick to listen so that we respond in the right way.

When we feel God leading us in a certain direction, the first and most important thing we need to do is test it against Scripture. This helps us make sure it is really God speaking to and leading us. God's voice will never say something that goes against the Bible. His voice is always consistent with the truth of his Word.

God wants to lead us, and he uses these three things—the Bible, people, and his voice—to direct us in life. They work in tandem with each other, so it's important that we make room in our lives for each of them. I encourage you to take some time at the end of this chapter to open your heart to God's leading. If we want to stay on the best path for our lives—God's path—and sidestep some of the potholes in life, then we must be willing to follow God as he leads us. As we do, we receive the supernatural strength and direction we need to make our way through life.

"For You, O Lord, are my Lamp; the Lord lightens my darkness. For by You I run through a troop; by my God I leap over a wall. As for God, His way is perfect; the word of the Lord is tried. He is a Shield to all those who trust and take refuge in Him" (2 Sam. 22:29–31 AMP). Even in the dark, surrounded by obstacles, God can and will make a way to keep moving forward as we follow him and rely on his leading in our lives.

20

Total Surrender

The greatness of a man's power is the measure of his surrender.

William Booth

Our family once had this crazy dog named Harriet. She was a black-and-white, wirehaired terrier, and if anyone bent down to pet her, she would leap up and knock them over. She grabbed socks out of the dirty laundry and could shred an entire roll of toilet paper in a matter of seconds. She was short, stocky, and strong. Harriet killed moles in our backyard. She smacked her food when she ate and even burped when she was finished! While she wasn't very ladylike, we still loved her.

Our biggest struggle was keeping up with her—Harriet was always a flight risk. If the outside door was open the slightest bit, she would squeeze through and take off as fast as she could, running down the street at the speed of lightning.

As frequently as she dashed out the door, I'm surprised she never got lost or hit by a car. After a whole lot of chasing her on foot, we finally discovered a trick. We figured out that if Leslie or I would quickly get in the car and start the engine, all we had to do was back the car down the driveway and Harriet would immediately run to us. She would jump in the back of the car as if it were her chariot sent to bring her home.

As soon as she hopped into the car, she was happy as could be. Someone watching us would think we were being lazy or had discovered a novel way to walk our dog. It was so funny to see Harriet run at breakneck speed and then just stop suddenly when she heard our car. No calling or chasing needed, just the sound of the engine was enough to bring her back.

Out the Door

I'm convinced that sometimes we act just like Harriet. We ask God for his advice and counsel about our lives and daily decisions, but then we start looking for another way. The second we see an open door, we run as fast as we can in whatever direction we please with no regard for the danger that might be out there. Too often, we act as if God wants to imprison us when really he's only trying to protect us.

The Bible is full of awesome promises about God being our protector and our deliverer. We know that God wants to rescue us and deliver us from times of trouble. We've seen a certain truth throughout our exploration of the Lord's Prayer, and we see it again here: Certain things initiate a God response in our lives. Psalm 91, one of the greatest passages on God's protection and deliverance, talks about not only the deliverance he offers but also some of the things that move him to come to our rescue. The entire psalm is amazing, and I encourage you to check it out, especially when you need to remind yourself of God's protection. But I want to shine a spotlight on one particular part of it:

> *Because he has set his love upon Me*, therefore I will deliver him; I will set him on high, *because he has known My name.* He shall call upon Me, and I will answer him; I will be with him in trouble; I will deliver him and honor him. (Ps. 91:14–15 NKJV, emphasis mine)

Here we see two things that cause God to act on our behalf. First, the passage says God delivers us when we set our love upon him. When we're focused on him as the passionate priority of our hearts, God is drawn to our cry when we call out to him. If my wife or children call me and tell me they're in trouble, I drop everything and act immediately. While I would help anyone, even a stranger, who asked, when it's someone I love, I don't even stop to think about it. There's something about setting our hearts and extending our love to God that cause him to want to intervene on our behalf.

Second, God is moved when we know his name. The Amplified version puts it this way: "I will set him on high, because he knows and understands My name [*has a personal knowledge of My mercy, love, and kindness—trusts and relies on Me*, knowing I will never forsake him, no, never]" (Ps. 91:14–15, emphasis mine). Knowing the Father's heart toward us enables us to trust and rely on him, and that causes God to respond on our behalf and lift us up. Clearly, there is a powerful connection between our being devoted to God and his hand of protection rescuing and delivering us.

What I've found is that often we're hesitant to rely on him because we don't truly know and understand his character. If we did, we'd be much more willing to let go of our own plans and exchange them for his plans.

The Lord's Prayer holds a key action that we need to take if we want to see God deliver us. That action is *surrender*.

It's one of the greatest secrets to living a significant and truly successful life. As we surrender, God delivers us—from our fears, our uncertainties, and our temptations. If we want to be rescued and delivered, we must be willing to let go of control.

Put Your Hands Up

The word *surrender* means to yield and to place yourself under someone else's authority. If you've ever watched an old western on TV, then you know the universal sign of surrender is to put your hands up. It's a sign of releasing control.

This is exactly the position we need to take with our lives as we surrender them to God. We say, "Here's my life, God. I'm letting go of all my efforts to control things. I'm not in charge. God, you are in charge." When we surrender, we place our will under his will. We place our opinions under his opinions, our desires under his desires. So often we want God to rescue us and deliver us, but we don't want to surrender. We want to hold on to control and do things our way.

In our journey with God, we discover that surrendering is not a one-time event but rather an ongoing process. In each season of our lives, there will be many occasions when we'll have the opportunity to surrender our will to God's. Sometimes surrendering means taking something precious to us and letting it go because God requires it. As painful as it may seem at the time, we must let it go, take our hands off, and walk away in order to make God our number one priority. It may be a relationship or a business, an old stubborn habit or a grudge we've held on to for too long.

On the other hand, sometimes surrendering to God means persevering with something he's called us to do. If he asks us to hold tight, then we must press on and not give up, no matter how difficult the task. As much as we want to run, we must surrender our will and make a commitment to stay at it no matter the cost. We must choose to allow God to accomplish something on the inside of us and not quit before he's finished. When we do this, we are surrendering to God's work in our lives.

I Surrender All

When we surrender, we're standing in line with a great company of people who have gone before, including Jesus. Before he was crucified, Jesus struggled with what had to come next. There in the Garden of Gethsemane, a place where olives were pressed, Jesus felt the full weight of the pressure that had been building around him for some time. Gethsemane was indeed a place of pressing for Jesus. As much as he knew what he needed to do, he still wrestled with the thought, *Could there be another way?* He even told the Father, "If you are willing, take this cup from me." But then he finished by saying, "Yet not my will, but yours be done" (Luke 22:42).

We all encounter these pivotal moments when God leads us to a point and then asks us to surrender. We need to choose whether we will lay aside our own will, lay down our plans, and embrace the path he is asking us to take. Will we run out the door like Harriet to pursue our own direction, or will we follow him?

While we should always live with purpose and vision, if there comes a point when we sense that God's plan is different from our own, the best thing we can do is surrender our plans and submit our will to his. God's deliverance, protection, and rescue are released in our lives when we surrender our personal agendas.

The Bible provides a powerful illustration of this principle in the book of Jeremiah. God's people are in a desperate situation; they are starving and about to be defeated by the Babylonians. Hearing their cries, God speaks to Jeremiah about how the people can be rescued and delivered. The prophet then goes before the king and tells him, "This is what the LORD God of Heaven's Armies, the God of Israel, says: 'If you surrender to the Babylonian officers, you and your family will live, and the city will not be burned down. But if you refuse to surrender, you will not escape! This city will be handed over to the Babylonians, and they will burn it to the ground'" (Jer. 38:17–18 NLT).

Listen to what the king says next: *"But I am afraid to surrender. . . . Who knows what they will do to me!"* (Jer. 38:19 NLT, emphasis mine).

Surrender went against the king's plan. It didn't make sense, and he couldn't see how it could possibly work out in his favor. This is often the way we respond when faced with a crossroads situation. Just like the king, we say, "Who knows what will happen to me if I surrender?" God offers us a way of escape, a plan for protection and deliverance, but we are afraid to surrender.

One of the reasons we don't want to give in and relinquish control to God is that we are fearful. But fear will destroy our momentum very quickly. Fear makes us focus on the what-ifs and forget the possibilities. We may be fearful about how things will turn out, what we might miss out on, or the price we may have to pay if we do indeed surrender. The truth is that *not* surrendering costs us far more in the end. Many times, our saving is in our surrender.

Surrender is counterintuitive to us in many ways—it often goes against what we think is best. But if we really want to find God's plan and *his* best for our lives, we must be willing to trust God enough to hand over control. If we don't, we're setting ourselves up for a life that will fall short of all God intends for us.

Thanks but No Thanks

God tells us that his thoughts and ways are immeasurably higher than ours. Our best-laid plans can't rival his plan for our lives. If we don't surrender to him, we step outside the boundaries of his grace and protection, making us vulnerable. When we linger in our stubborn pride, we delay our own progress and create a kind of friction that can bring our momentum to a halt.

Sometimes we're stuck in a season and no matter what we do we can't escape it. We can't figure out why we can't move ahead. Sometimes it's the fact that we're subtly resisting God, and we're left spinning our wheels, unable to get out of the rut we're in. When we resist surrendering to God, we usually end up miserable, anxious, frustrated, and striving rather than experiencing the grace and flow of God's momentum.

Our prideful, human nature wants to be in control and have its own way. When God asks us to surrender to his plan, we often say one thing but then do another. We say, "Thanks, God—of course, I want to follow you." But then we're off on our own direction faster than Harriet bolting out the door. Despite the right words and maybe even good intentions, our actions say, "Thanks, but no thanks, God. I'm good. I've got this." That's not what it looks like to be devoted to God and to rely on him.

I've found that my plans and God's purposes don't always fit together nicely. Even when he's given me a goal or a dream, the way he chooses to carry it out usually ends up different from the way I thought it would be. In fact, at times I've gotten so frustrated by a situation that wasn't working out that I pushed and pushed only to find out later that God had a different plan all along. In hindsight, I could see that if God had answered my prayer the way I thought he should have, it would have been a disaster. That's why it's so important that we be willing to make surrender a part of our lives. We don't know what's best, and we don't see the big picture. But God does. When we surrender, we relax and allow God's power to lift us and carry us to safety.

Even when we may not have all the answers or understand where God is leading us, we can rest in knowing that he knows more than we do. He sees the end from the beginning and every step along the way.

Most Likely to Succeed

When our lives, our plans, our purposes, and our futures are surrendered to God, we are in a position to be more and accomplish more than we ever dreamed. Until we surrender, though, our potential for significance is limited to what we can accomplish in our own ability. We may be able to accomplish a lot, but with God, we can accomplish so much more.

When we pray, "Your will be done," we acknowledge, like Jesus in Gethsemane, that God's purpose and plan are perfect no matter how they may appear or make us feel in the moment. Pursuing success as the world around us defines it may seem so attractive. The lure of money, fame, success, career achievements, and the approval of other people will always appeal to our selfish nature. Every time the door opens, we may want to bolt and go chasing after these flashy temptations. But even if we get everything the world has to offer, what have we truly gained?

When all is said and done, our earthly successes won't last and our achievements won't satisfy. Only Jesus offers us eternal satisfaction. His plans for our lives are the only ones that can bring true fulfillment deep within. He gave us the Lord's Prayer not as a magic formula or words to be memorized but as a model for how we can experience the astounding, supernatural power of a life lived in surrender to our Father's plans. Your life was created with purpose, designed to have unique significance on this earth. The starting point for fully realizing that divine purpose and significance is releasing our lives completely to our Father. True significance is found in surrender.

One step forward: Heavenly Father, I open my heart and my life to your leading. Guide me forward in the direction that you would have me go. Help me to trust you and follow you every step of the way. I believe that you have good plans for my life, and I want to live a life that has true significance. Protect me and keep me strong so that I can come through life's trials, temptations, and challenges a stronger person with a better understanding of who you are. Help me to fully release my life to you—my plans, my dreams, my future—so that I can accomplish something far better: your plans and purposes for my life. In Jesus's name, amen.

Conclusion

Forward with Our Father

Let us not cease to do the utmost, that we
may incessantly go forward in the way of
the Lord.

John Calvin

A few years ago, I took a trip to Durban, South Africa. It was
shortly after we had started our first international church
campus there, and a couple of guys and I went to visit and
encourage our team. Durban has some incredible beaches and
has become one of the surfing capitals of the world. While
standing on the beach taking in the beautiful views, Jared,
our worship pastor, told us a hilarious story about his prior
visit to Durban when he had been on a college missions trip.

Having always wanted to learn how to surf, he was determined to try. He's a pretty athletic guy who played sports
his whole life and, in fact, went to college on an athletic
scholarship. So he thought, *How hard can it be?*

Jared was staying with members of a local church, so on their day off, he asked his host if they could go surfing. They set out early the next morning, grabbing a couple of borrowed surfboards on the way. When they got to the beach, the waves were cresting around eight feet. They found a spot between two large piers and started paddling out to the highest waves, which was a pretty good distance to swim.

As they were paddling out, Jared turned to the other guy and said, "Okay, man, tell me what to do." His new friend said, "I don't know—I've never been surfing before. I think you just stand up." It wasn't exactly the response he was hoping for, but Jared was fairly sure he could figure it out.

However, he had no idea about the strength of the current. They were trying to get out to the waves, but the current kept pushing them back and to the side, making it difficult for them to make progress. About halfway to their goal, the other guy gave up and went back to the beach.

Jared was determined to keep trying. But after a few more minutes, he noticed he wasn't really moving forward or getting closer to his goal. In fact, he was slowly drifting to his left, the current pushing him closer and closer to the giant concrete piers. The massive columns of each pier were covered in barnacles. Jared had lived in Florida, so he knew that the razor-sharp barnacles could cut him to pieces if a wave slammed him into a pier.

After about an hour, extreme fatigue and, consequently, fear set in. The current kept getting stronger and pushing him closer to the barnacle-covered pier, and he was only getting weaker and weaker. Strong as he was, he knew he wasn't strong enough to fight the current much longer.

Finally, a lifeguard spotted him, realized the trouble he was in, and came after him. He threw Jared a life preserver and told him to stay on his surfboard. The lifeguard then proceeded to swim around the pier, pulling Jared behind him to safety!

As relieved and grateful as he was, Jared felt incredibly embarrassed. Crowds of people had started gathering to see what was going on, and the fishermen on the pier were shouting and swearing at him because he had scared away all the fish. The most embarrassing part, though, was being towed back to shore by a lifeguard who swam the entire way, pulling him along behind as if it were nothing.

Just listening to Jared describe the scene he caused that day had me and the other guys almost crying because we were laughing so hard. Who would have thought one guy trying to surf could cause such an ordeal!

Jared later found out that if he had only changed his direction, he wouldn't have been fighting the current and would have been able to swim out of danger without a problem. He had stubbornly persisted in trying to move forward, swimming against the current, and it had gotten him nowhere but into trouble.

Bound and Determined

Sometimes we find ourselves swimming through life just like my friend Jared. We have a goal in mind, and we're bound and determined to reach it. Sometimes we push so hard trying to achieve it that we exhaust ourselves and make no progress. There's nothing wrong with having goals, but sometimes we insist on going our direction even though we're clearly not achieving any forward momentum. We fail to realize that our plan may not be in the same direction as God's best for us.

As long as Jared kept trying to swim in the direction he thought was best, he remained in danger. His rescue came when he allowed someone to lead him in a direction that was completely different from the one he'd been trying to go on his own. Often we get stuck in place because we're not willing to switch directions and follow God's plan for our lives. If we want to move forward, to experience the momentum for which we were created, then we must return to our starting place in the Lord's Prayer.

When Jesus taught the disciples how to pray, he began, "Our Father." To truly connect with God in prayer, we must begin and end with remembering that God is our Father. Relating to God as our loving Father is the greatest key to moving forward and building momentum in our lives. It changes everything else. If we're not connected to God as our Father, we've missed out on the most important thing, and the Lord's Prayer becomes nothing more than a collection of words.

Our Father's Love

I don't know what your relationship with your earthly father was like. Maybe it was good and healthy, and he was a great model of all that a father should be. Maybe you didn't have a dad, or if you did, maybe it wasn't a good relationship. Or more likely, it was a mixed bag of some good and some bad things coming from a loving but imperfect man. For better or worse, we tend to think about God in the way we saw our earthly father.

With this in mind, I want you to know that God is a loving, gracious, patient father. He's slow to anger and quick to forgive. He's gentle and full of mercy. He isn't distant, and he isn't a tyrant who demands that you be perfect in order to be loved and accepted. He loves you just the way you are right now. This is awesome news for everyone, because none of us is perfect.

Yet he is also just. He's a perfect, holy God. He has a standard of what separates us from him. No matter how hard we try to live good lives, we all fall short of God's standard because we've all sinned (Rom. 3:23). When Adam and Eve disobeyed in the Garden of Eden, sin entered the world and all of humanity lost their direct relationship with God. But he created us, he loves us, and he longs to have a relationship with us. He doesn't want to be separated from us. That's why he sent Jesus.

The Bible says that Jesus came in the form of a man and walked this earth, the same earth we're walking today. He was tempted in every way so he could fully relate to us, but he never gave in to the temptation and therefore lived a sinless life. He became the sacrifice for our sins on the cross. All of the things we have ever done wrong or will do wrong, all of our mistakes, all of our sins—past, present, future—were placed on Jesus on the cross. He took our place—yours and mine—on that cross. After he was crucified, he was laid in a tomb, and three days later, by the power of the Holy Spirit, he rose from the dead.

The Bible teaches that through the cross we receive forgiveness from our sin and through Christ's resurrection we have new life—a new beginning, a fresh start. It says, "If you confess with your mouth, 'Jesus is Lord,' and believe in your heart that God raised him from the dead, you will be saved. For it is with your heart that you believe and are justified, and it is with your mouth that you confess and are saved" (Rom. 10:9–10). These verses give us the practical steps to a fresh start with God.

Willing to Believe

It starts with believing. In our hearts, we believe God loves us and sent Jesus. We believe that Jesus gave his life on the cross and rose from the dead. We may not fully understand it all, but something inside our hearts says, "This is true." When we believe in our hearts, then we can confess with our mouths. We pray and declare our love for God and invite his presence into our lives. From that moment, our lives are changed. The Bible says we are reborn or saved, adopted into God's family, and united with our Father through Jesus Christ.

Obviously, the word *saved* is a Bible word. You may have never heard it, or maybe it carries some baggage for you. It simply means "to be pulled out." I always tell people to picture themselves in a war zone, in the middle of a firefight, buildings on fire, utter chaos. You're standing there, defenseless, not sure what to do. Then all of the sudden you hear a helicopter fly in, and out of nowhere a rope ladder comes down and offers you a way of escape. Picture this from a spiritual perspective, and you get an idea what it means to be saved. We're "pulled out" from an eternity spent in darkness, saved from a purposeless life here on earth, a life without peace and so many other things.

Another word the Bible uses to describe what happens when we receive Jesus into our lives is *salvation*. When you salvage something, you rescue it from being discarded and thrown away. God wants to rescue us and fulfill within us the incredible destiny he created us for, but we must be willing to let him lead us.

I'm not sure where you are on your journey. Maybe your relationship with God is strong and growing. Maybe you don't remember ever praying a prayer, asking God to forgive you through Jesus Christ and to come into your life. Many people I meet don't recall making that decision. It doesn't mean you haven't been to church or haven't read your Bible, but those things don't make you a Christian. You become a Christian when you choose to accept Christ—when you deliberately believe in your heart and confess with your mouth.

Maybe at some point in your life you did pray and receive Christ, but if you were to be honest, today your life isn't on track with God. You may have made some choices that caused you to fall away from a relationship with God. Maybe unintentionally over time you just drifted away, and you know in your heart you need to renew your relationship with God.

Fresh Start

The great news is that God stands before you with arms wide open. The Bible says that he loves you with an everlasting love, which means his love never ends. He can and will forgive you of anything you ask. In fact, I encourage you, if you're reading this right now and you know you need a fresh start with God or you don't really know where you stand in your relationship with him, to take a minute to pray this prayer.

Father God,
    Thank you for the amazing plan you have for my life. I'm coming to you today, asking that you would fill me with your presence and give me a fresh start. Thank you for sending your Son, Jesus, to die on a cross for me so I could receive forgiveness from my sin. I believe that Jesus was raised from the dead so I could have new life. Forgive me of my sin, cleanse me, and make me new. Live inside me and give me the strength to live for you. In Jesus's name, amen.

If you prayed that prayer and meant it with all your heart, you just made a fresh start with God. It's a life-changing, amazing step. Second Corinthians 5:17 tells us, "Now we look inside, and what we see is that anyone united with the Messiah gets a fresh start, is created new. The old life is gone; a new life burgeons!" (Message). One of my favorite verses describing the fresh start process is Colossians 1:13: "For he has rescued us from the kingdom of darkness and transferred us into the Kingdom of his dear Son" (NLT). It's pretty amazing to think that a spiritual "transaction" has just happened. Your life is now in God's hands.

If you just made a fresh start, I encourage you to keep moving forward. Making a fresh start is an incredible step. But it is just the first of many that God wants you to take as he leads you forward on this amazing journey. Keep taking your next steps. Like Paul, set your eyes on the goal of pressing on to finish the race well and receive the heavenly prize. There's so much more to life than what you see here on earth. Run the race and live this life with eternity in mind. Let this be a moment when you "re-up" your commitment to making progress and being all that God has called you to be.

You don't have to remain stuck in place, swimming upstream against the current. Follow your Father, and he will build tremendous forward momentum in your life as you pursue this incredible adventure with him. Remember, God has an amazing future in store for you!

Notes

Chapter 2 Honor Code

1. "Truett Cathy's Five-Step Recipe for Business Success," http://www.tru ettcathy.com/about_recipe.asp (accessed September 14, 2012).

Chapter 4 Honor Opens Doors

1. Robert Frost, *The Road Not Taken, and Other Poems* (New York: Dover Publications, 1993), 1.

Chapter 5 Your Kingdom Come

1. C. S. Lewis, *The Great Divorce* (New York: HarperCollins, 2001), 75.
2. C. S. Lewis, *Mere Christianity* (San Francisco: HarperSanFrancisco, 2001), 135.

Chapter 6 Make Up Your Mind

1. Jennifer Read Hawthorne, Jack Canfield, and Mark Victor Hansen, *Life Lessons for Loving the Way You Live* (Deerfield Beach, FL: Health Communications, 2007), 96.
2. "Positive Thinking: Reduce Stress by Eliminating Negative Self-talk," Mayo Foundation for Medical Education and Research, May 28, 2011, www.mayoclinic. com/health/positive-thinking/SR00009/NSECTIONGROUP=2.
3. Janet Rae-Dupree, "Can You Become a Creature of New Habits?" *The New York Times*, May 4, 2008, www.nytimes.com/2008/05/04/business/04unbox.html.
4. Marc Kauffman, "Meditation Gives Brain a Charge, Study Finds," *Washington Post*, January 3, 2005, www.washingtonpost.com/wp-dyn/articles/A43006 -2005Jan2.html.

Chapter 8 Time for a Change

1. See http://www.betterhealth.vic.gov.au/bhcv2/bhcarticles.nsf/pages/Anger
_how_it_affects_people.

2. William J. Cromie, "Anger Can Break Your Heart," *Harvard University Gazette*, September 21, 2006, www.news.harvard.edu/gazette/2006/09.21/01-anger.html.

Chapter 9 Our Daily Bread

1. Brian Tracy, *Maximum Achievement: Strategies and Skills That Will Unlock Your Hidden Powers to Succeed* (New York: Fireside, 1995).

2. Connie Prater, "Poll: Credit Card Debt the New Taboo Topic," GfK Roper Public Affairs and Media for CreditCard.com, www.creditcards.com/credit-card-news/talk-about-credit-cards-the-new-taboo-1276.php.

3. Danny Kofke, "One in Four Americans Would Not Inform Spouse of Financial Difficulties," One Money Design, October 25, 2011, www.onemoneydesign.com/one-in-four-americans-would-not-inform-spouse-of-financial-difficulties/.

4. See http://www.nscblog.com/personal-growth/the-monkeys-fist-an-ancient-parable-for-modern-times.

Chapter 10 In God We Trust

1. Roy B. Zuck, *The Speaker's Quote Book: Over 5,000 Illustrations and Quotations for All Occasions* (Grand Rapids: Kregel Academic & Professional, 2009), 343.

Chapter 12 Enough Is Enough

1. Joyce Meyer, *Enjoying Where You Are on the Way to Where You Are Going: Learning How to Live a Joyful Spirit-led Life* (Tulsa: Harrison House, 1996).

Chapter 15 Locked Up

1. Zuck, *The Speaker's Quote Book*, 201.

2. Fred Luskin, *Forgive for Love: The Missing Ingredient for a Healthy and Lasting Relationship* (New York: HarperOne, 2007), 32.

Chapter 16 Locked Out

1. Corrie Ten Boom with John and Elizabeth Sherrill, *The Hiding Place* (Grand Rapids: Chosen, 2006).

John Siebeling is lead pastor of The Life Church, a thriving, ethnically diverse 7,000-member multi-campus church in Memphis, Tennessee. He is a member of the Board of Directors for ARC (Association of Related Churches) and is a widely respected peer of other well-known ARC pastors. The Life Church has a weekly television program with over 125,000 viewers on average weekly. John has twenty plus years of ministry experience, including several years serving alongside his wife as missionaries to Kenya.

JOHNSIEBELING.COM

twitter: @johnsiebeling

Find out more about John Siebeling, stay up to date, check out videos, and get great resources for you, your church, or your ministry at **johnsiebeling.com**.

> **Fresh Start Resources**

> **Message Series**

> **Books & Music**

> **Make Room Conference**

> **The Life Church TV**